CRICKET CONTRASTS

CRICKET CONTRASTS

From Crease to Commentary Box

Jim Laker
with Pat Gibson

Stanley Paul
London Melbourne Sydney Auckland Johannesburg

Stanley Paul & Co. Ltd
An imprint of the Hutchinson Publishing Group
17–21 Conway Street, London WIP 6JD

Hutchinson Publishing Group (Australia) Pty Ltd
16–22 Church Street, Hawthorn, Melbourne, Victoria 3122

Hutchinson Group (N Z) Ltd
32–34 View Road, PO Box 40–086, Glenfield, Auckland 10

Hutchinson Group (S A) Pty Ltd
P O Box 337, Bergvlei 2012, South Africa

First published 1985

©Jim Laker 1985

Set in Linotron Baskerville 11/12pt
by Input Typesetting Ltd, London
Printed and bound in Great Britain by Anchor Brendon Ltd,
Tiptree, Essex

ISBN 0 09 159760 9

Contents

Acknowledgement

When I decided that I should need the cooperation of a leading cricket journalist to complete this book, I looked no further than my old friend and *Daily Express* colleague, Pat Gibson. I am delighted that he agreed to work with me and I owe him a sincere vote of thanks. His reliability, conscientious approach and above all his great love of our game has again been very much in evidence over the past few months.

Photo Acknowledgement

For permission to reproduce photographs, the author and publisher would like to thank Patrick Eagar, *Daily Express*, Central Press, Press Association, Sport & General Press Agency, Reuters and Vivian Jenkins.

Foreword

Laker's Wonderful Year
by Neville Cardus

Against the Australians in 1956, J. C. Laker bowled himself to a prominence which might seem legendary if there were no statistics to prove that his skill did indeed perform results and deeds hitherto not considered within the range of any cricketer, living or dead.

No writer of boys' fiction would so strain romantic credulity as to make his hero, playing for England against Australia, capture nine first-innings wickets; then help himself to all ten in the second innings. Altogether, 19 for 90 in a Test match. If any author expected us to believe that his hero was not only capable in one chapter of a marvel as fantastic as all this, but also in another chapter, and our earlier chapter, bowled a whole Australian XI out, 10 for 88, the most gullible of his readers would, not without reason, throw the book away and wonder what the said author was taking him for.

Yet as far back as 1950 Laker was hinting that he possessed gifts which on occasion were at any moment likely to be visited by plenary inspiration and accomplish things not only unexpected but wondrous. At Bradford, five miles from his birthplace, Laker, playing for England v The Rest, took 8 wickets for 2 runs in 14 overs – a feat which probably the great S. F. Barnes himself never imagined within mortal bowler's scope – or even desirable. Against Nottinghamshire at the Oval in 1955, Laker took 6 wickets for 5.

Between 1947 and 1953 he did the 'hat trick' four times.

Obviously the gods endowed him in his cradle with that indefinable power which from time to time generates talent to abnormal and irresistible achievement. And he has done his conjurations – they have been nothing less – by one of the oldest tricks of the bowler's trade. Not by the new-fangled 'swing' and not by 'googlies' or Machiavellian deceit by flight through the air, has Laker hypnotised batsmen into helpless immobility, but by off-breaks of the finger-spin type which would have been recognised by, and approved by, cricketers who played in Laker's own county of Yorkshire more than half a century ago. He really follows the great succession of Yorkshire off-spinners – from Ted Wainwright, Schofield Haigh, not forgetting F. S. Jackson, to George Macaulay, reaching to Illingworth of the present day.

Laker's actual finger spin probably has seldom been surpassed on a 'sticky' or dusty wicket, in point of velocity and viciousness after pitching. I can think only of Ted Wainwright, Cecil Parkin and Tom Goddard who shared Laker's ability to 'fizz' the ball right-handed from the off-side. There was more temper in Macaulay's attack than there is in Laker's, more vehemence of character. But for sheer technical potentiality, often for sheer actual spitefulness, Laker's off-spin must be regarded as entirely out of the ordinary, and very much his own.

Any great performer needs to be born at the right time. If Laker had begun to play for Surrey in the 1930s, when wickets at the Oval and on most large grounds were doped and rolled to insensibility, he might have made one or two appearances for Surrey, then vanished from the scene. Or maybe he would have remained in Yorkshire where pitches were never absolutely divorced from nature and original sin.

Laker was clever, too, to begin playing cricket and bowling off-spin after the alteration to the lbw rule dangerously penalised batsmen who had brought to a fine art the use of the pads to brilliant off-breaks pitching off the stumps and coming back like a knife – as Cecil Parkin's frequently did. Laker has been quick to adapt his arts to the deplorably unresourceful footwork of most batsmen of the present period; moreover he has, with the opportune judgement of those born to exceptional prowess, taken advantage of the modern development of the leg-trap.

On a good wicket, his attack naturally loses sting. His tempting slowish flight enables – or should enable – batsmen to get to the pitch of his bowling. He thrives on success in perhaps larger measure than most bowlers. He likes, more even than most bowlers, to take a quick wicket. There is sometimes an air of indolence in his movements, as he runs his loose lumbering run, swinging his arm slowly, but with the flick of venom at the last split second. At the end of his imperturbable walk back to his bowling mark he stares at the pavilion as though looking for somebody, but looking in a disinterested way. He is entirely what he is by technique – good professional technique, spin, length and the curve in the air natural to off-spin. He does not, as Macaulay and Parkin did, assert his arts plus passion of character and open relentless lust for spoils and the blood of all batsmen.

He is the Yorkshireman, at bottom, true enough; but southern air has softened a little the native and rude antagonism. Even when he is 'on the kill' on a wicket of glue there is nothing demonstrably spiteful in his demeanour; he can even run through an Australian XI in a Test match, as at Manchester in his 'wonderful year', and seem unconcerned.

His bowling is as unassuming as the man himself and on the face of it as modest. That's where the fun comes in; for it is fun indeed to see the leisurely way Laker 'sends' his victims one after another, as though by some influence which has not only put the batsmen under a spell, but himself at the same time. Somebody has written that all genius goes to work partly in a somnambulistic way. Jim Laker is certainly more than a talented spinner.

By permission of *Wisden Cricketers' Almanack*

1

For Better, for Worse

The older I get, the better a cricketer I seem to become.

People remember the great days – such as when I took eight wickets for two runs in the England Test Trial at Park Avenue, Bradford, in 1950 and 19 wickets for 90 against Australia at Old Trafford, Manchester, in 1956. But they tend to forget that there were bad days too – such as when I finished with match figures of three for 206 as Australia reached a record 404 for three to beat us at Headingley, Leeds, in 1948 and when I took two for 154 facing that great West Indian triumvirate of Weekes (206), Worrell (167) and Walcott (124) at Port-of-Spain, Trinidad, in 1954.

Cricket is unique in this respect: no other sport seems to live so much in the past, glorifying the old, disparaging the new. When I was playing, grown men would come up to me asking me for my autograph for their sons; nowadays small boys approach seeking my signature for their dads! And although it is now more than a quarter of a century since I played in my last Test match, I find myself in greater demand than I have ever been.

In recent years, I have been as far afield as Auckland, New Zealand, and Cape Town, South Africa, just to speak at cricket dinners. I have arrived in Edinburgh in deepest winter to find cricket fanatics travelling 30 miles or more through several feet of snow to hear me talk about the game. And I have now found myself part of a new cricket phenomenon – nostalgic evenings hosted by Brian Johnston which have attracted huge audiences all round the country. One February night at Bristol, getting on for

11

2,000 people were at the Colston Hall to hear Tom Graveney, Ray Illingworth and myself yarning about the old times. In other words, there were twice as many people ready to turn out on a winter's evening to listen to us talk about the game than seem prepared to sit in the sun and watch some of the greatest cricketers of the day actually playing the game against Gloucestershire!

I am not complaining. Cricket's grip on the public's affection has enabled me to make a reasonable living as a television commentator, newspaper columnist, after-dinner speaker, raconteur even – all roles in which I never quite envisaged myself when I was playing. But I do think that we need to get things into perspective. And that is why I want to use my own career to illustrate just how much the game of cricket has changed during the past 30 years.

Some things have changed for the better; some for the worse. And while these developments have inevitably changed the character of cricket and cricketers, I consider myself lucky to have enjoyed the best of both worlds.

For today's cricketers live in a different world from the one I knew during my playing days. Now, sponsors seem to provide for their every need from the cars which they drive to the equipment they use, not to mention the clothes they wear both on and off the field. Then, I travelled to my first Test match at Lord's on a no. 157 bus. I had to buy all my own clothes from shirts and trousers down to socks and jock-straps. And the only equipment I was ever given was one bat per season.

Now, England players are paid upwards of £1,500 for appearing in a Test match, thanks to the magnificent sponsorship of the Cornhill Insurance Company, and more than £10,000 for going on an overseas tour. Then, I received £75 for my first Test – plus a third-class rail ticket to get there from the preceding county match – and £300 for my first tour.

As an illustration of the enormous difference in remuneration, I have worked out that after 13 years in the game I earned £15,070 – made up of £2,370 for playing in 29 Tests, £2,700 for five overseas tours and £10,000 for

13 seasons with Surrey – though I was fortunate that my benefit in 1956 coincided with my taking those 19 wickets against Australia at Old Trafford, as a result of which I managed to make as much as £11,000. At present rates of pay, 29 Test matches (£43,500), five tours (£50,000) and 13 years on a county's staff (£117,000) would bring in a grand total of £210,500. And these days a beneficiary of international standing would be very disappointed if he did not get at least £60,000.

Obviously the cricketer of the fifties was desperately underpaid, despite the fact that we were quite accustomed to playing in front of crowds of 30,000 in County Championship matches. It was not that the counties were mean and miserly. It was simply that players' salaries came solely from gate receipts since there was no such thing as sponsorship let alone the massive share-out of money now received from television and radio.

Having said all that, I must make it perfectly clear that I do not begrudge the blokes one new penny of what they earn today – providing they are good enough to earn it. Players like Ian Botham, David Gower and Bob Willis are fully entitled to the kind of money that comes their way. They have reached the top of their chosen profession and, having done that, there is no reason why they should not be paid as much as the stars in other sports, like tennis, golf and football.

No, there is no jealousy in my mind – for the simple reason that if I had my time again I would choose to play at the time I did play. It was a friendlier game then, for a start. On the field, it was fiercely competitive but we seldom went over the top, as they seem to do so often now, in our reaction to success and failure. Ungentlemanly conduct, bad manners, dissent – call it what you will but it is not nice to see. Off the field, too, there seems to be a growing churlishness in players' attitudes, especially towards the Press and, indirectly, the public, since they are the people they represent. I had my share of publicity – good, bad and indifferent – at a time when reporters hounded the players to a far greater degree and had to learn to live with it. Once you have become a famous sportsman, not to say a superstar, you must expect to come under close scrutiny from the media.

If it was easier to accept that in the fifties, then I think it is also fair to say that it was easier to become successful than it is now.

The main reason for that was the state of the wickets, which, many people tend to forget, invariably govern the way the game is played. There is no question that, by and large, wickets were a lot better then than they are now. It is very seldom these days, even in Test cricket, that you find a pitch where the bounce is regular, very seldom that a bowler of any class cannot get movement off the pitch – hence the great temptation for captains to persevere with quick bowlers to the detriment of the spinners.

So why should this be? Well, for economic reasons, ground staffs have been very severely reduced and there is now an acute shortage of experienced, top-class groundsmen who have mastered an art that requires long years of apprenticeship. At the Oval, they used to need 20 men just to push the five-ton roller. Now one man can simply sit there motoring slowly up and down the pitch.

Given good wickets and fine weather, batsmen – with far more opportunities than they get today since 60 first-class innings in a season were not unusual – were able to thrive. Yet there was ample compensation for the bowlers when the rain came down. Pitches were left uncovered and I for one became a better bowler because of that. The skills developed trying to get batsmen out on good wickets meant that bowlers often became almost unplayable when conditions were in their favour. And the confidence gained from collecting a crop of wickets made them all the better when it came to bowling on good pitches again.

Similarly, a batsman could strike three or four bad wickets on the trot but console himself with the thought that it would not be long before he got the chance to make a stack of runs on good ones. Such a situation may not have produced better cricket. But I think it produced better cricketers and certainly fairer contests.

Another important factor in the way the game has changed is the cricket ball itself. My old Surrey and England colleague Alec Bedser has a collection of cricket balls used 30 years ago which bear little relation to the kind of balls they have today. They were all hand-made and hand-polished – and within a matter of 20 overs the shine would have disappeared despite all the efforts of the bowlers who used to rub them on their trousers just as frantically as they do now. The seam would soon have been flattened and in places like Brisbane and Barbados the cover would have changed colour from red to brown with little pieces coming out of it from contact with the rock-hard pitch. And there was no question of the fielding side having the ball changed. That just did not happen in those days.

How different it is now. The making of cricket balls by hand is one of the old crafts that has disappeared – again for economic reasons – and we are in the age of machine-made cricket balls coated with polyurethane which retain their shine and seam throughout a full day's play. And still the bowlers are not satisfied, judging by the number of times they want the ball changed.

With the wickets and the balls in their favour, it is just as well that the no-ball law was changed a few years ago, otherwise it would be totally impossible to bat at all against the kind of fast bowling barrage we are now accustomed to seeing from the West Indies. It is bad enough having to contend with their fearsome pace, dangerous bounce and disconcerting movement off the seam and through the air – but at least they only bowl from 22 yards. Under the old law – which was geared to the back foot being behind the bowling crease rather than the front foot behind the batting crease, as it applies now – they would have been really lethal!

'Dragging' – not to mention 'chucking' – got so bad on England's 1958–9 tour of Australia, when we lost 4–0, that I went out to the middle at the Sydney Cricket Ground to measure exactly where fast bowler Gordon Rorke was landing with his left foot. It was four feet in front of the batting crease, and since he also had an enormous drag it meant he was letting the ball go at the batsman from about 18 yards! And I well remember Colin Cowdrey's remark when one of his clerical friends called to see him.

'Colin,' said the reverend gentleman, 'you are making the mistake of always getting on to the back foot against Rorke.'

'I'm frightened of playing forward to him', explained Cowdrey, 'in case he treads on my toes.'

For all that, I am still convinced that it was an easier game to play in those days – and particularly on tour. They were much longer trips since we went to countries like Australia and South Africa by sea. But at the end of a long, hard season in England, it was really luxurious to put your feet up for three or four weeks on what was virtually a holiday cruise. Once we had three weeks' net practice before we even played a match. And for those who did not strike form straightaway, there were plenty of opportunities to catch up on a tour designed to give everyone plenty of cricket.

My sympathies are very much with the present-day cricketers who find themselves being flown to the other side of the world and expected to play within hours of their arrival. Then, if they don't make an immediate hit, there is so little cricket between Tests and one-day internationals that they are virtually condemned to the roles of drinks waiters and supporters for the rest of the tour. In a way, the players have only themselves to blame since to pay them what they expect means getting the best possible return from their services in terms of revenue. But it does not make their lives any easier.

I am sure that it is not so pleasant playing the game these days, either. Crowds have changed, whether they are in Melbourne or Manchester, Christchurch or Kingston. They are much noisier – as many television viewers are often writing to complain – and far less patient, probably because a growing number have been brought up on the action-packed one-day game and have little time for the intricacies of Test cricket. And there is a disturbing new element, especially in England. Whereas people used to go to cricket matches primarily to watch the game and enjoy the occasional pint of beer with their friends, many now seem to be more attracted by the licensing hours that allow them to drink all day and use the cricket as an excuse.

Yes, all things considered, I am glad I played the game when I did. But that does not mean that I do not still derive tremendous enjoyment from my involvement in it from schoolboy level as president of the Surrey Schools' Cricket Association through county cricket as chairman of Surrey's Cricket Committee right up to Test matches in my work for the BBC and the *Daily Express*.

Being a Yorkshireman, I was born into cricket and nothing has ever happened to change my opinion that there is something about the game which you do not get in other sports. Basically, I suppose, I put team games way ahead of individual pursuits and I think the spirit of comradeship engendered by the game of cricket endures far longer than in probably any other activity.

It may be because cricket is such a great leveller. You can throw together eleven cricketers from vastly different backgrounds – whether it's an English public school or a coal miners' welfare club, a Barbados beach or a Bombay back street – and you will very rarely find any serious disagreement between them. In the dressing room, the main topic of conversation will always be cricket. And for anybody deeply involved in the game, it becomes a way of life.

There is nothing to beat playing the game. But what I have enjoyed more than anything else since I retired is that I have been able to keep in touch with so many old players, colleagues and opponents alike, with whom I might easily have lost touch years ago.

If I go to Trent Bridge, for example, I can look forward to having a beer with Joe Hardstaff. If I go to Australia, I know I will be renewing my acquaintance with the likes of Arthur Morris, Ray Lindwall and Neil Harvey. In Barbados, there will be a welcome waiting from Everton Weekes. In New Zealand, Bert Sutcliffe will revive memories of when we played together during the war.

17

And whenever I return to Yorkshire, I am forever bumping into old cricketers with whom I played as a boy.

An awful lot has happened since then, not just to me but to the game of cricket. And if you have borne with me thus far, perhaps I can tell you what I have made of it all.

2

Birth of a Cricketer

Rumour has it that overnight rain followed by a drying wind allowed the thumb to go down a good inch on a spin bowler's length at Bradford Park Avenue on 9 February, 1922. A couple of miles or so away in a small terraced house, I first saw the light of day. But that coincidence would not have meant a thing to my fairly substantial family, none of whom knew very much about the peculiar Yorkshire religion called cricket which was to become my way of life.

I was the fifth child but the first son of a truly remarkable lady who was eventually to complete 50 years as a full-time yet unqualified schoolteacher. She celebrated her forty-fourth birthday that year and, sadly, did not live to see me play first-class cricket. But she did see the back of three husbands.

My own father came second on the list. Born and bred in Sussex, he was a skilled stonemason whose work took him to Yorkshire. But I have no recollection of him whatsoever and have never even seen a photograph of him. Indeed, I had no knowledge of his demise until two years ago when, after some diligent research, the former England and Middlesex cricketer Peter Parfitt discovered his final resting place in a tiny village churchyard close to Barnoldswick. He had never had any connection with the game of cricket; nor had anyone else in the family.

Life was far from easy for my mother in those days. My earliest and vaguest memories are of her taking me – then aged about two – into various classrooms and telling me to sit quietly as she went about her work for the

19

princely sum of between three and four pounds a week. By the age of five, I had been accepted at the local council school at Frizinghall, and it was during the next five years that my fanaticism for football and cricket was firmly established.

There was no money for such luxuries as a cricket bat and it took weeks and weeks of chewing through half-penny packets of gelatine lozenges to collect one hundred coupons before I finally returned home in triumph with my very first bat. And what service it provided during those long summer holidays! There was no question of the family going away anywhere for a proper holiday, but I was never interested anyway. Every morning at nine o'clock, I would set off for Northcliffe playing fields in the company of a couple of other enthusiasts, clutching my precious bat and a ball of some description. Then, with our jackets as the stumps, we would play whole Test match series with sessions that went on for hour after hour and day after day. It was, of course, the only sensible way to spend a holiday.

Fortunately my school work did not seem to suffer and at the age of ten I delighted my mother by passing a grammar school scholarship and winning a free place at Salts Boys' High School where I was to spend seven of the happiest years of my life.

The financial situation had improved slightly with the arrival of a stepfather and subsequently we moved to a new house in a pleasant part of the village of Baildon. But throughout those years, my life was confined to little more than a ten-mile radius around Bradford. A choir trip to the Lake District and a few days at Filey are the only times I can remember leaving the district until I was 16, when I went on the kind of journey that had seemed beyond my dreams – all the way to Eastbourne to stay with my sister, Doreen. Needless to say, Yorkshire were playing Sussex at the Saffrons at the time!

Educational standards at Salts were terrific but sporting standards less so – which probably explains why I appeared to be outstanding at football and cricket. Soccer was undoubtedly my first love. School games were played on Saturday mornings and then I would be off hot foot down to Valley Parade, paying my sixpenny admission to the schoolboys' section of the Spion Kop to support my beloved Bradford City. I can still reel off the entire side of the mid-thirties when crowds of 20,000 used to pack in to see the Paraders. Nowadays they are one of the many clubs struggling for their very existence and down to the faithful few, but I still go and watch them whenever I get the opportunity.

It was in the three or four years before the 1939–45 war that three people, in their different ways, sowed the seeds for what has been the fullest of careers – indeed the fullest of lives.

First, there was Alf Burgoyne, secretary of Saltaire Cricket Club. He had noted my performances on the school cricket field, just down the road from the club ground at Roberts Park, and was keen to register me. By the age of 16, I was making my first-team debut, but although there could be no better grounding for any aspiring cricketer than the tough, highly competitive Bradford League, I was no budding world beater. In fact the records show that in the 50 games I played in the league, I scored only 526 runs and took just 79 wickets. In nine years as Saltaire's professional, the great Sydney Barnes took no fewer than 904 wickets at 5.2 runs each!

Still, the limited amount of promise I had shown was quite enough to set my mother into action. With her savings stuffed into her handbag, she took me off to Herbert Sutcliffe's shop in nearby Leeds. The best Stuart Surridge autograph bat in stock was mine at a cost of 45 shillings. Then came the accessories – a pair of real buckskin pads which I used throughout my first-class career and still have to this day, boots, socks, shirts, even a box and batting gloves. It is frightening even to contemplate what she had to go without herself to afford such extravagance on me.

Mother also discovered that the great Yorkshire opening batsman held coaching lessons indoors at Headingley throughout the winter and I was booked in with the other young hopefuls. In most cities, it would seem a

21

bit strange to see a 16-year old trudging through the snow at Saturday lunch time with a cricket bat under his arm, but it did not bring a second glance in Leeds. Years later when I returned to Headingley to play in a Test match, Herbert was quick to remember those days.

'What a pity your mother never lived for this day,' he said to me. 'She really was a remarkable woman.'

Around that time, I had struck up a very firm yet somewhat odd friendship with one Harry Dolphin, a nephew of the outstanding Yorkshire wicket-keeper Arthur Dolphin, who was unlucky to play only once for England. It was a bit odd in that Harry was almost 15 years older than me and worked as a freelance journalist. But he was a pure cricket nut and we were almost inseparable for about four years until I went into the army.

It was like suddenly discovering a doting, elder brother and Harry taught me more about the game of cricket than the combined efforts of those Yorkshire legends George Hirst, Herbert Sutcliffe and Emmott Robinson. He was terribly upset when I was shipped out to Egypt and immediately volunteered for overseas service himself. His troopship was torpedoed on his way out to join me and he was one of hundreds posted missing, presumed drowned.

My schooldays ended in 1939 and armed with credits in matriculation I succeeded in getting a job with Barclays Bank in Bradford. Two years there provided a tough introduction to the world of commerce. For a monthly salary of £5, I worked from 8.30 am to 6 or 6.30 pm on weekdays and even on Saturdays balance time was never before 1.30 pm. And I had to attend Bradford Technical College five nights a week in winter to study for banking examinations.

In summer, it was always hit or miss whether I got to the ground in time for my Bradford League fixture. But there was a war going on and though a good many of my acquaintances had gone for ever, I could not wait for the call.

Calling-up age was 20 and it took a good deal of persuasion before I finally managed to convince my mother that I should volunteer. Then, having given a false age, I was soon on my way to do eight weeks' infantry training at Earl Shilton in Leicestershire. That was followed by a posting to Chilwell at Nottingham, where, it was said, anyone with any real ability at football or cricket was set for the duration.

A funny story that turned out to be! Within weeks, I was issued with tropical kit and sent home to Yorkshire on seven days' embarkation leave. The 'old lady' was distraught and, much to my embarrassment, spent half that week pounding the doors of every officer she could find complaining about the injustice of an under-age soldier being dispatched overseas with such haste. I was much relieved that her efforts were all in vain because I was secretly looking forward to the adventures that lay ahead.

Before the summer ended, I had bade her farewell, never suspecting that it would be four long years before I would see her again. We boarded the *SS Mooltan* in Glasgow late one evening and next day I was counting more than 20 ships in convoy escorted by an aircraft carrier, a battleship and destroyers *en route* to the Middle and Far East.

We spent eight weeks at sea in the most primitive and hideous circumstances. By 5 pm, everyone had to be below decks where in my particular section 300 men were sleeping wherever a space could be found, sharing 20 wash basins and half a dozen lavatories. We took a zig-zag course across the Atlantic dodging the U-boats, spent a week marooned in Freetown Harbour, enjoyed four days of unadulterated luxury in Durban and finally disembarked in Port Said. And it was there, a world away from my native Yorkshire, that I was to make the most important decision of my cricketing life.

Four years in a non-combative unit is basically a cushy number and as the months slipped by I began to make the most of it. I started by creating something of a name for myself in army soccer matches and before very long had gained a place in the British Army XI, playing along-side the likes of the great Tom Finney, Scotland's Willie

Telfer, Harry Clifton from Newcastle United, big Dave
Massart of Birmingham and George Male of Arsenal.

But it was in 1942 when I played my first game of
cricket for what seemed like an age that I made a startling
discovery which was to lead to me becoming one of the
most famous sportsmen of the age. All the matches were
played on matting wickets and I decided to experiment
by bowling a few off-spinners. Harry Dolphin had
suggested it a few years earlier, and now, in my twenty-
first year, I began to practice at every opportunity. There
were no coaches to help, no manuals to study as I became
a self-taught off-spin bowler in the shadows of the Sphinx
and the pyramids.

To my utter amazement, I was soon turning the ball
quite prodigiously on the coconut matting strips. Wickets
galore came my way in inter-unit games and one haul of
eight for 30 at the famed Gezira Sporting Club earned
me a place in all the representative matches. This meant
I was rubbing shoulders with a whole host of eminent
cricketers, including Dudley Nourse from South Africa,
Bert Sutcliffe, Don Taylor and Tom Pritchard from New
Zealand and several English Test players, including Peter
Smith, Norman Yardley, Tom Dollery and George
Emmett.

Towards the end of my long stay in the Middle East,
a fine stadium was opened in Cairo and appropriately
named the El Alamein – and it was there towards the
end of the summer of 1944 that I played in a two-day
'Test' match for England against Australia in front of
about 10,000 troops.

We spent a steaming hot day in the field on the
Saturday and I was foot-sore and weary at close of play
as I made my way over Kasr-el-Nil back to my unit with
an enormous pack of cricket gear on my back. Halfway
across the bridge, a dispatch car with flags flying pulled
up beside me and out popped the head of a hoary old
brigadier who looked as though he had the desert sand
embedded in his bristling moustache. By that time I had
reached the exalted rank of War Substantive Corporal,

24

but I was utterly amazed when he offered me a lift into town.

I had no sooner jumped in alongside him than he turned to me and asked where I had come from. In all innocence, I told him I was just on my way back from Alamein.

A look of approval swept over his face. 'By God, Corporal,' he exclaimed excitedly, 'tell me, what's the position there now?'

I hesitated, realizing that I had done it all wrong. 'Well, sir,' I said at length, 'Australia were 320 for eight at the close of play but we missed a few chances.'

Suddenly his face turned a nasty purple colour. The car stopped abruptly. And Corporal Laker was left to continue his journey on foot.

At least I had held my own with some of the best on the field. And for the first time I was beginning to believe that when the war was over I might just have an outside chance of playing county cricket.

In April 1945, I had another stroke of luck, though a month later I wondered if it was just fate. By a 1,000-to-one chance, my name came out of the hat for four weeks' leave in the UK and in next to no time I was back in Bradford – after a quick dash through the Mediterranean and a brief skirmish with a U-boat in the Irish Sea.

I had not realized how tough it had been at home. Times had changed. My stepfather had gone the way of all flesh and our comfortable Baildon home had come under the hammer. My mother, at 67, was still teaching and had just managed to buy herself a tiny, terraced home close to the Bradford City football ground.

She had paced up and down Spring Gardens all day long, impatiently awaiting my return, looking hard at every soldier who appeared. We had both changed, too. The shy, nervous, 19-year-old private who had left home was now a seasoned, 23-year-old army sergeant. And she looked tired, though that was not altogether surprising since she had been refereeing a school soccer match the day before.

The month flew by and I seldom left her side until, a

few days before my leave was due to end, she suggested I should go down to Eastbourne to spend a couple of days with my sister. Perhaps she had a premonition because she insisted on accompanying me to the station – and by the time I reached the south coast she had returned home, collapsed and died.

It took a good deal of negotiating before the Army authorities agreed to extend my leave for a further two weeks to cover the funeral, though it seemed a sheer waste of time for me to return to Egypt. The war in Europe was over, peace treaties had been signed – and, in any case, I was shortly due for repatriation. But there was some compensation when I returned to my unit and found I had been selected to represent the MEF (Middle East Forces) against the CMF (Central Mediterranean Forces) in a two-day game to be played at 51 Rest Camp in Rome.

For most of us, it was the first time we had flown, and what a baptism it turned out to be. We were cramped in total darkness in the bomb bays of a wartime Liberator which took five hours to find Italy and a small runway at Foggia. And as if that was not bad enough, we then bounced around in the back of a truck for what seemed an eternity before finally checking in at our destination.

I thought we had a very useful side, skippered by Norman Yardley and including Peter Smith, Bert Sutcliffe and Don Taylor – but it was quite a reunion for our senior players when we met up with the opposition. Among their ranks were George Emmett, Tom Dollery, Arthur Wellard, Pat Vaulkhard of Derbyshire and Phil King of Lancashire; our two Kiwis met up again with Tom Pritchard; and, for the first time, I met Arthur McIntyre who was to keep wicket to me at Surrey for so many years.

Apart from the fact that we played on a matting stretched tight over a concrete base that produced a wicket which was lively in the extreme, my memories of the game are fairly vague. I do recall that we got a hammering and there were grave doubts about the legality of my two wickets, both lbw much to the disgust of the batsmen.

Strangely, I have a much clearer recollection of our visit to the Opera House in Rome where the great Gigli was singing in *Cavalleria Rusticana*. Bert, Don and myself missed our scheduled flight back to Cairo and decided to move on and have a look at war-torn Naples. We slept where we could and discovered the only decent food was in the New Zealand NCO's Club where my northern accent was a big problem as I was masquerading as a warrant officer from Wanganui! Cash was running short and our leave well overdue when we dropped in at a Naples airfield and found an old Dakota about to take some cases of fruit to Egypt. Perched on orange boxes and feeling horribly airsick, we finally made it back to Cairo West via Malta and Tobruck.

It was then simply a question of seeing out my time before returning to the UK towards the end of 1945. But the next few months turned out to be the most frustrating of my entire army career. The war was over but the process of demobilization dragged on and on.

After a short spell in Leeds, I was posted in deep midwinter to Folkestone with its ice and snow, biting east winds and zero temperatures. I had a month of sheer misery there until I pulled a few strings and got a transfer to the relative comfort of the War Office. In London, I moved into digs at the home of a long-time Army pal, Colin Harris, in Forest Hill, where I was to stay for five years, accepted almost as a son in the closest-knit and happiest family I have ever encountered.

The start of the 1946 season found me playing services cricket up and down the country, but I also joined Catford Cricket Club with whom I enjoyed a great deal of success. And it transpired that my performances had been noted by Surrey, who asked me to play in a trial match against the Wanderers at the Oval. I still had a few lingering doubts about my ability to make the grade at county level, so I was more than surprised when I was offered a professional contract, to take effect from my demobilization date in August.

I was in a quandary. London seemed to be *the* place to be and with this mind I had already written to Barclays Bank and requested a transfer to the capital on my release and this had been granted. But in addition, General Palmer, who was in charge of Army cricket, had begged me to consider a move to the Regular Army with the promise of a permanent peace-time commission.

Financially there was little to choose between all three offers but money never really entered my head. I resigned from the bank, thanked the general for his kind offer and accepted the Surrey contract at terms of £6 per week for the following winter to be supplemented by match money in the summer months.

Having taken the plunge, I was determined to succeed and figured that the way ahead lay in assiduous practice and rigorous training. A no. 58 tram to Dulwich and from there a no. 37 bus to Wandsworth took me week in and week out through the winter to Alf Gover's famous cricket school.

I had struck up a firm friendship with Arthur Phebey, who was also on demobilization leave from the Fleet Air Arm and about to join Kent. We played golf together whenever possible and 'The Phebe', who had won amateur soccer honours with Dulwich Hamlet, took me along to some of their evening training sessions.

There was no time to waste. When I reported to the Oval for my first full season as a professional cricketer in the middle of April 1947, I was already in my twenty-sixth year, and at that age you don't really want a protracted spell playing club and ground or even Minor Counties cricket.

By early July, I had established my place in the first XI. A county cap followed in August and by the end of the summer I had topped the bowling averages with 79 wickets at 17.97 runs apiece.

And to crown a remarkable first season I was a late selection for the MCC tour of the West Indies under Gubby Allen. I was on my way.

3

The Way We Were

Whenever I go racing, I am forcibly reminded of what it used to be like to earn one's living as a cricketer. The sight of jockeys having to bow and scrape to their supposed superiors – the owners and trainers – in the paddock takes me straight back to the days of amateurs and professionals in cricket. The removal of any distinc-' tion between the 'gentlemen' and the 'players' remains the best thing that has happened to the game in my lifetime.

I always thought that such class distinction was positively ridiculous. And I still think it is positively ridiculous to see a living legend like Lester Piggott doffing his cap to a man for whom he may be making something like half a million pounds a year. One respects a person for what he does rather than who he is and I would far sooner have doffed my cap to a professional like Len Hutton than an amateur like E. R. T. Holmes.

Errol Reginald Thorold Holmes was my first captain at Surrey and, quite frankly, the biggest snob I ever met. Like Douglas Jardine, whom he had succeeded as captain in 1934, he played in a Harlequin cap and was a magnificent batsman on good wickets. But he could not play the off-spinner – which was very fortunate as far as I was concerned. I could bowl him out in the nets just as soon as he came in and I am sure that was one of the main reasons why I got so many early chances.

I was a bit of a rarity at the Oval in those days since it was unusual for anyone born outside the county to play for Surrey, let alone a Yorkshireman. You did not get players transferring from county to county as frequently as you do now, but because of the war, which had ended only two years earlier, I got a special registration which allowed me to play straightaway. Yet I was readily accepted by the senior professionals – the likes of Alf Gover, Tom Barling, Bob Gregory and Stan Squires – when I reported for pre-season practice.

There was no such thing as a fitness programme; none of the circuit training or callisthenics you see today's players indulging in. A bowler was simply expected to bowl in the nets from 10.30 in the morning until 6.30 at night every day for about three weeks. And then he had to go out again in the evening to bowl at any club members, young amateurs mostly, who fancied a net. None of the professionals relished that very much, and you used to find the quicker bowlers trying to knock the batsmen's heads off so they would not stay too long!

It was hard graft but I was very enthusiastic about it, believing – unlike a lot of the players – that it was important to practice properly. I don't think it made us as fit as players are nowadays with their rigorous training schedules. But I do believe that batting techniques were better because batsmen practised so much. And I am sure that bowlers were a good deal stronger because they did a lot more bowling. Certainly you did not get fast bowlers breaking down with such alarming regularity as England's have done in recent years.

One very down-to-earth reason for that may have been the boots we wore. All our equipment was vastly different, of course, starting with those old-fashioned flannel trousers and shirts which soon became heavy with sweat. But if they were a bit of a burden to carry around all day, I shudder to recall the weight of the boots in which I bowled for most of my career. It is marvellous to put on a pair of modern cricket shoes which feel like carpet slippers and one appreciates the comfort. But I cannot believe they give the same support around the ankles and tendons that our heavy old boots used to do. They must have made us a lot stronger in the legs – and so did all the walking we did.

There were not too many motor cars about – in fact I

did not own one myself until I was nearly 30 – and in any case not even the amateurs were allowed to drive themselves to matches. But that was about all we did have in common on our travels. Take a visit to Leicestershire at Grace Road, for example. The twelfth man and masseur, who were in charge of the baggage, would be allowed to take a taxi from the Oval to St. Pancras Station with all the equipment. The amateurs would also take a taxi. The rest of us would go by underground. At St. Pancras we would meet up as a team again, but only briefly before the amateurs went off to their first-class compartment. Our tickets were third-class. On arrival at Leicester's Midland Station, the amateurs would take a taxi to the Grand Hotel. The baggage party would load up another taxi. And the professionals would start walking down the road to look for the Stag and Pheasant. We were paid three or four pounds extra for an away match and that would cover the bill for four nights there, including bed, breakfast and evening meal.

In the mornings, we would make our way to the trolley-bus station and take a twopenny trip up to Grace Road and then walk the rest of the way to the ground. The amateurs would duly arrive by taxi. And the first time we would see them again was when we actually walked out onto the cricket field.

Such class distinction was never a good thing for the game and because I thought it was totally wrong I was probably considered a bit of a rebel. Not that we had a stream of amateurs at the Oval, unlike some of the other counties who would have a lot of schoolmasters coming into the side during the summer holidays. Apart from Errol Holmes, we had Peter May, who was very much the amateur cricketer when he first came into the side, and of course Stuart Surridge, who, while always being a true amateur in the sense of the word, was more like a semi-professional because he was always one of the boys.

Yet Surrey was probably the last county to dispense with separate dressing rooms for amateurs and professionals and it took even longer for the club hierarchy to come to terms with the new order. I never went into the committee room for 20 years. In fact I only just about knew where it was. I hardly knew any members of the committee, apart from the then president, H. D. G. Leveson Gower – and for two years he thought I was Laurie Fishlock!

Whenever I bumped into the president, or 'Shrimp' as he was known in the dressing room, he would call out, 'Good morning, Laurie', and I would reply, 'Good morning, sir'. Apart from the fact that Laurie was 20 years older than me and was a left-handed opening bat with a bald head, I suppose we were very similar!

Still, at least Errol Holmes knew who I was as a result of our encounters in the nets. And his belief in my ability as an off-spinner was rewarded on 6 August 1947, a date imprinted on my memory and on a cricket ball which is still one of my most treasured possessions. It was the first time I took five wickets for Surrey, though the portents were not encouraging as we travelled south to play Hampshire on the United Services Ground at Portsmouth. On the train from Waterloo, we discovered that Alec Bedser and Alf Gover had both got 99 wickets and all the talk was about who would be first to reach 100. Portsmouth was reputed to have the greenest wicket in the country and when Errol Holmes won the toss he had no hesitation in putting Hampshire in to bat. They opened with the Rev. J. R. Bridger and Neville Rogers, and in truth they never looked like getting out until, in desperation I think, Errol Holmes eventually tossed the ball to me. Almost immediately, it began to turn and after bowling the reverend through the gate with an off-break early on I went on to take the first seven wickets and eventually finished with eight for 69. I cannot remember now whether it was Alf or Alec who was first to 100 wickets, but I do recall that it was well into the third afternoon by the time either of them struck.

Naturally I was over the moon, or whatever the expression was in those days, and was further excited, by the prospect of playing Middlesex the next day at the Oval; everybody wanted to play in a fixture that would draw a 25,000 crowd on the Saturday. Then, in the last hour of the Hampshire game, I was fielding in the gully to Gover when I tried to stop a fierce cut and dislocated the top of my spinning finger. I left the field in tears because I would not be able to play against Middlesex.

Next day, Middlesex won the toss, batted first and made 537 for two declared on a belting pitch. Syd Brown was their only 'failure' with 98. Jack Robertson made 127, Bill Edrich 157 not out and Denis Compton 137 not out. Stuart Surridge took one wicket and Eric Bedser the other. And as I sat in front of the pavilion watching Compton go on to bowl us out twice on a turning pitch to give Middlesex an innings victory, I began to realize what the game of cricket was all about.

Defeat was not uncommon for Surrey that season. The side that was to win the County Championship for seven years in succession had begun to take shape but it was three more years before everything fitted into place. Alec Bedser was just about established as England's leading bowler but the retirement of Alf Gover in 1947 left an enormous gap. We badly needed another opening bowler and for a while there was nobody in sight. In addition, Stan Squires died in 1950 at the age of 41, Bob Gregory retired and Tom Barling had just about reached retiring age too. But people like Tom Clark, Bernard Constable and David Fletcher had developed into useful batsmen, and when a young boy called Tony Lock began to fulfil his promise and another called Peter Loader emerged from Beddington Cricket Club to become one of the best new-ball bowlers I ever saw, the time was ripe.

All we needed, then, was the appointment of Stuart Surridge as captain to bring everything to fruition. He will go down in the record books as a fairly ordinary cricketer, though in fairness his performances were always a little bit better than he was given credit for. If you look back, he took around 500 wickets in his career and managed to hang on to about 50 catches at short leg every season. So you could not really label him a passenger.

But it was as a captain, a leader of men, that he was one of the most dynamic characters ever to set foot on a cricket field. He did not believe it was possible for Surrey to lose a match. As a result, he made a few mistakes, but not very many. He was also the greatest retriever of lost causes I have known. And he had the happy, inborn knack of knowing how to handle individuals.

One has to remember that this side, which eventually contained ten Test cricketers, included some very differing temperaments and personalities. To get the best out of everybody is not an easy thing – as some other captains have discovered in recent seasons. Yet Stuart could handle Lock and he could handle Laker, both in different ways. He would shout and bellow at Locky, but he knew it was useless to shout and bellow at me. Similarly, he got on extraordinarily well with such contrasting characters as Alec Bedser and Peter Loader. All in all, he was a very popular guy, even in the professionals' dressing room.

That was hardly surprising, I suppose, when you consider some of his stunts, or, as they so often turned out, acts of genius. The most memorable of them came in 1954 when Surrey beat Worcestershire by an innings and 27 runs at the Oval in a three-day match that was all over in little more than five hours.

Play did not start until 2 o'clock because of overnight rain. Then Stuart put Worcester in to bat on a wet wicket – pitches were not covered in those days, of course – and Locky and I bowled them out for 25 with their last seven wickets falling for just five runs. An hour before the close, we had reached 92 for three – 67 ahead – with Peter May going well on 31, the wicket apparently easing and most of us sitting on the balcony with our boots off and our feet up. Suddenly we heard our idiot of a captain on the amateurs' balcony upstairs clapping his hands to declare and a few minutes later Surridge was marching into our dressing room to find it in a state of panic with people hurriedly getting dressed or searching for their boots. I will always remember Alec Bedser looking at him and saying: 'Skipper, you've got to remember that somebody else can play this game as well as us.' To which Stuart replied: 'Nonsense. We've got enough. We'll bowl them out again.'

Out we went again to take two more wickets that night,

and inside an hour next morning we had claimed the remaining eight. It would have been over quicker if I had not pointed out to Surridge when they were 26 for eight that we had all got our 100 wickets for the season, except Loader, who had 99. 'Give him a bowl', I urged, 'so he can get the last one or two.' Surridge agreed, but instead of taking me off, as I had expected, he took off Lock whose match figures at that stage were six wickets for five runs. With the ball still turning, I had the problem of bowling at the last two Worcester guys without getting them out. The only way I could do that was by bowling full tosses outside the leg stump and I had been whacked for two or three fours and they had reached 40 before Loader eventually got his wicket.

Amazingly, we had won by an innings in under a day's cricket. And we were sitting in the dressing room reflecting on it all when Stuart came bursting in, shouting 'Well done, well done.' Again Alec Bedser looked at him and said: 'You are a golden boy, a lucky so-and-so, you really are.' Again Stuart had an answer: 'Well, you might say that, but I did ring the met. office before I declared and the forecast was diabolical.' It seems incredible now but it was soon pouring down with rain and if we had not got it over so quickly we would never have achieved a result in that game.

That performance was typical of Stuart Surridge's initiative and imagination, which were never more evident that in the run-in to our third successive County Championship. With ten matches left, we were eighth in the table, 46 points behind the leaders, Yorkshire. But then we won nine of those last ten games, five of them inside two days, to take 112 points out of a possible 120 and win the title by 22 points from Yorkshire.

Much was made of the fact that Laker and Lock, both of us having been left out of the forthcoming MCC tour of Australia, picked up 103 wickets during that period at an average of less than nine runs apiece. But that was only half of the story. Alec Bedser topped our bowling averages that season with 89 championship wickets at 13.30 and Peter Loader, who made his England debut in

the final Test against Pakistan, took 100 wickets in a
season for the first time.

Alec Bedser was simply born to be a great medium-
fast bowler. Everything about him was made and
fashioned for the job. His solid, 6ft. 3in. frame, his enormous strength and his economical run-up of seven or
eight big strides were ideal; his body action was copybook,
everything it should have been; his control was supreme.
But what made him the best bowler of his type I have
seen was that, unlike most inswing bowlers, he had the
very rare ability to make the ball swing in late, towards
the end of its flight. Normally an inswing bowler comes
in with an open-chested action – New Zealand's Lance
Cairns is a prime example in recent years – and the ball
swings in from the moment it leaves his hand. Alec would
often start it about a foot outside the off stump and it
would not duck in towards the middle stump until the
last two yards of its flight.

That was enough to make him a formidable bowler in
any company. But he went on to add a second weapon
to his armoury which made him one of the truly great
fast-medium practitioners. This was his leg-cutter which,
again, was a little bit different to the leg-cutters you
see bowled today. Alec's was a special kind of delivery,
somewhere between a cutter and a spinner, and was
particularly useful on a damp wicket, that is to say on
the sort of pitch which normally caused the medium pacer
to be replaced by a spinner. Alec had such gigantic hands
that he could put his fingers across the seam, almost like
anyone else holding a ping-pong ball. Then he would pull
his second finger down the seam and almost make the
ball seam rather than cut at medium pace. Such was his
superb control that he could pitch this leg-cutter on
middle stump and consistently move it away a matter of
four or five inches. With that kind of ability, it is hardly
surprising that he tends to be a little critical of modern
players and their techniques.

In contrast to Alec Bedser, Peter Loader did not look
as though he had the physique to make it as a fast bowler
when he joined the Surrey staff from club cricket at

Beddington. Tall and wiry, Scrubs – as we christened him because his hair reminded us of a scrubbing brush – seemed doomed to failure. But when I watched him in a couple of second XI games, I was immediately impressed by the way he could swing the new ball. Subsequently he developed excellent control and a marvellous change of pace. He could always bowl – though some people used a different verb! – a very good bouncer and he had a slow off-spinner which, again, was a bit suspect. But the great beauty of his bowling remained his consummate skill with the new ball.

I can vividly recall a match against Nottinghamshire on a very good pitch at the Oval when he took eight wickets for next to nothing by constantly bamboozling the batsmen with his powers of swing and control. It is generally accepted that you bowl an outswinger from close to the wicket and an inswinger from the edge of the return crease. But I can remember watching Loader that day and marvelling at what I saw. He ran up and bowled one ball from close to the wicket that was a perfect outswinger. The batsman played and missed. Next ball, Loader ran up and bowled from the edge of the crease – and with the batsman looking for the inswinger this time, the ball pitched on middle stump and hit off. Loader was just as capable of bowling an inswinger from close to the wicket so it was a sheer waste of time for the batsmen to look to the bowler's feet – as most of them do – for an indication of which way the ball was going to swing.

Loader's biggest problem remained his physique. He was never a big guy and old Scrubs tended to live life to the full so that if he was asked to come back and bowl late in the afternoon the ravages of previous exertions would take their toll. But in my view he was a supreme artist with the new ball and possibly the best new-ball bowler I have ever seen.

With such talent at Stuart Surridge's command, it is perhaps not surprising that we were so successful, or that some counties seemed to have an inferiority complex when they played against us. Many was the time we were put in to bat purely as a defensive measure because the opposition were frightened to bat themselves. But we had our critics, too. There was plenty of dark whispering about the legality of the bowling of Tony Lock and Peter Loader; some counties, notably our arch rivals Middlesex and Yorkshire, who were not used to being runners-up to anybody, did a lot of carping about the Oval wickets. And there were plenty of people who said that we did not have the greatest batting side in the business.

I will admit that there were grounds for suspicion about some aspects of the bowling of both Lock and Loader. But a lot of research over the years enables me to refute any allegations about Surrey rigging the Oval wicket in our favour. Apart from Guildford week, we played all our home games at the Oval, yet of the 1,944 wickets I took during my career, only a third of them were taken there. In fact, my personal record was better at Lord's, which was supposed to be a pretty good wicket in those days. And I could name a dozen grounds, some of them overseas, which were more generous to me than the Oval.

As for Surrey's batting, it is perfectly true to say that we did not have the best line-up in the country, though Peter May, of course, made a tremendous difference when he came into the side. He was our one class batsman until Ken Barrington and Micky Stewart established themselves during our run of success. But we had Bernard Constable, Tom Clark and David Fletcher who were all sound, solid players, and Arthur McIntyre, the wicket-keeper, would get fifties and sixties with a fair amount of regularity. In any case we often felt that we did not need to score gigantic totals because we were such a good bowling side. 'We don't want to waste our time scoring 400,' Stuart Surridge would say. 'We'll get 270 and bowl them out for 90.'

That was Surrey in the Fifties, a side bred on success like the Arsenal of the thirties or Liverpool today. We always went out trying to win, indeed expecting to win. If we did not, a few people in the dressing room would have something to say. There would be moans and arguments, but most of them were off the field and that was the important thing.

38

4

Staying On . . . and On

When I retired from first-class cricket at the end of the 1959 season, I never imagined that a quarter of a century later I would still be totally involved in the game as a BBC television commentator and chairman of Surrey's cricket sub-committee. Indeed, I did not think I would have any more involvement at all when the publication of my book, *Over To Me,* in 1960 created such a storm of controversy that I was declared *persona non grata* at the Oval and had my honorary life membership at Lord's suspended by the MCC.

The sole reason for my retirement – announced on board the ship taking us to Australia for the 1958–9 tour – was the arthritic condition of my spinning finger. It had been getting gradually worse over the years and though I could have carried on playing at the highest level a bit longer than I did, it would have been on an irregular basis and I did not want to do that. Nor did I want to get involved in a full-time capacity as a professional in one of the leagues because I had just gone into business and could not spare the time.

I had plenty of offers from some of the top clubs in Lancashire and the Midlands, but it was Norton in the Staffordshire League who came up with a proposal that suited me very nicely. They did not want me to do any coaching at all, just play in 20 Saturday games plus two more on bank holidays at £60 a match with cash collections if I took five wickets or scored 50 runs. Only a year earlier, my Test match fee had been no more than £75!

The money was highly acceptable but it was not my

main motive for going back to play 'league'. I had always been a bit of a devotee of league cricket – and still am, come to that – because it was where I had started my career 20 years earlier. And I wanted to get the game back into perspective.

At Norton, my predecessor as professional was Frank Worrell and my successor Garfield Sobers, and obviously I could not match either of those two great cricketing knights as an all-rounder. Spinners, after all, have the most difficult task as league professionals since they tend to be more dependent on the kind of high-class fielding and catching that only comes with playing the game day in day out. And, on top of that, many of the grounds are so small that even a mishit which would have resulted in an easy catch at the Oval would often go for six. But, despite the problems, I thought I did reasonably well – and, far more important, I enjoyed the experience enormously.

One season was enough, though, because by then I was getting immersed in my business interests which were to become many and varied. I had started by putting some money into a knitwear business with an old friend of mine, working as a director from an office in Oxford Circus. Among other things, we introduced a line of Jim Laker sweaters and sports shirts, but in retrospect I think we made a mistake by doing it too early. Five years later, men's fashion knitwear was all the rage!

I went into printing, too, learning the basics of letterpress and litho with Roy (later Lord) Thomson's in Gray's Inn Road, and into sculpture, operating from a studio in Park Lane and producing bronze heads of a real cross-section of the well-known personalities of the day – from Jomo Kenyatta to Sir Alec Douglas-Home to Jackie Collins! Most of them, I recall, went to adorn the boardrooms of big companies in the City.

There was also an exciting venture with my old mate Arthur Phebey, the former Kent opening batsman. He was managing director of The Builder Ltd., and we became the first people to stage trade exhibitions on trains. We would hire the complete works from British

40

Railways, sell space to companies in the building trade, fit out all the carriages, including a hospitality wagon, and take it all around the country. It was the most interesting and stimulating job I had ever done.

Yet cricket, it seemed, would not let me go. One night – or in the early hours of the morning, to be more exact! – I found myself in deep conversation with Trevor Bailey. We were in Manchester with Denis Compton and Godfrey Evans in connection with some promotional work we were doing. But Trevor, as usual, was promoting Essex – and he must have been making a good job of it, for the following morning I picked up the *Daily Express* and was shocked to discover that I had agreed to play for Essex as an amateur.

The news came as something of a surprise to most of my associates as well, since my views about amateurs were well enough known. And since my controversial book had put me out of favour with most of the cricketing establishment, I don't think Trevor's announcement met with unanimous approval at Essex, either. But the more I thought about it, the more I felt that I had had enough of controversy. If Essex really did want me to play for them, then I would simply go and play.

Where we did make a mistake, perhaps, was in the way we arranged my playing schedule. It was agreed that I would play in one or two matches and then have the next one or two off to pursue my business interests. But when you are in your forties, you soon stiffen up after a spell of bowling and every time I went back to Essex it would take me at least one game to get properly loose again. Even so, I carried on like that for three seasons, before I finally finished playing first-class cricket and settled for the occasional game with the Rothmans Cavaliers, pioneers of televised cricket on Sunday afternoons which eventually led to the formation of the John Player League.

I felt I was still very much the businessman and it was a complete surprise when I received an invitation from the BBC that was to lead to a whole new career. They wanted someone with the kind of cricketing knowledge that can only be gained from playing at the highest level

41

to work alongside such established professional broadcasters as John Arlott, Brian Johnston and Peter West. I had never considered myself for such a job. Indeed I had never seen the inside of a commentary box until I made my debut on BBC2 at Fenners in April 1968.

To say I was nervous as Frank Bough opened the programme is putting it mildly. But then John Arlott turned to me and whispered: 'You'll be fine. Just imagine we are sitting together in the saloon bar of a pub, be natural and say whatever you think is right.' I have tried to follow his advice ever since.

My style must have appealed to somebody because it was not long before I was having to make another major decision. My commentary work was beginning to overlap with my involvement with Arthur Phebey and with the BBC keen to acquire my services on a more or less full-time basis it was obvious that I would have to choose between the train and the tube. Cricket commentating is a very concentrated job over a period of three or four months so for a large part of the year it is almost impossible to commit yourself to anything else. And that is obviously unacceptable to people who might wish to employ you.

It was around this time that the MCC restored my honorary life membership after a seven-year suspension, and with all forgiven at the Oval as well I had a call one day inviting me to become an ex-officio member of Surrey's public relations committee.

I was only too pleased to help my old club. And my commitment increased when they made me an honorary life member, a great accolade since it is even rarer than life membership of the MCC. There was also a feeling that if I was going to make a significant contribution I would obviously be more useful on the cricket committee than on the public relations side. Then, when Raman Subba Row found that his involvement at the Oval had become so demanding that he wanted to shed some of his duties, he asked me to become chairman of cricket. The wheel had gone a full circle. I do not think I would have accepted the job if Micky Stewart had not been installed already as cricket manager.

It is vital for any cricket chairman to watch most of the matches his club is involved in. After all, when you have to make decisions about hiring and, more important, firing cricketers, they would have a genuine grievance if they knew you had not seen them play very much. I see as much cricket at the Oval as I possibly can but when my TV commitments keep me away I know that I can rely on Micky to bring me up to date on every situation.

We have an excellent working relationship. And I am delighted to say that I am also graciously received in the dressing room as well. I like to believe that they, unlike some Surrey sides of the past, feel they are dealing with somebody of their own kind. In contrast to some of my contemporaries, I always avoid talking about the successes of the fifties, though naturally I am happy to oblige if anybody wants to ask me any questions or feels that I can offer a bit of advice.

It is not difficult to see some similarity between Surrey and Yorkshire in that both counties have failed to live up to their great traditions. But I think we have come to terms with our lack of success rather better than they have. And I was particularly pleased that while Yorkshire were tearing each other to pieces over the sacking and subsequent reinstatement of Geoff Boycott, we at Surrey were able to replace Roger Knight, a popular and respected captain for five years, with Geoff Howarth, our first overseas skipper, with the minimum of rancour.

Roger was as proud and sensitive as anyone in his position and it was not easy to persuade him that it was a good time to make the change – even though he had just accepted new responsibilities as a housemaster at Cranleigh School and was facing the additional pressures of a testimonial season. But in the end he was mature enough to agree to continue playing under Howarth, whose leadership qualities have played no small part in establishing New Zealand as a force to be reckoned with in Test and one-day international cricket.

There were other problems to be dealt with at the same

43

time, like Robin Jackman's decision to settle in South Africa which left a huge gap to be filled (he had, after all, taken 1,206 wickets for the county); like David Smith's sad departure over a matter of club discipline which cost us a player of England potential; like Monte Lynch's acceptance of an offer to join the rebel West Indian tour of South Africa which threatened at one time to cost us another one. As I write, we are hoping that Nick Taylor, son of former Yorkshire and England opening batsman Ken Taylor, will fill the Jackman gap, wishing Smith well with his new county, Worcestershire, and still wading through the mass of rules and regulations to try and establish just what Lynch's trip has cost him.

The question of where cricketers go in the winter seems to have become almost as important as what they do in the summer. Airline schedules, air fares, passports, visas – and sometimes for the wives as well as the players! – are complications that cricket administrators did not have to deal with in my playing days. Surrey's Jack Parker, I think, was one of the first professionals to think of taking himself abroad for some winter sunshine. But he did it by going down to Tilbury and working his passage on a ship to Australia, and came back the same way.

Still, there are certain pressures today that Jack did not have to worry about, either – from the marketing men. They are the people on the Oval staff who keep the club solvent. And, quite rightly, they are always pointing out that the task of raising half a million pounds a year would be a great deal easier if they could point to a measure of success on the field. This is the message we try to get across to our players: those guys are paying your wages, so you must play your part by giving them a decent product to sell.

The other priority, of course, is the development of players. And in that respect I believe that my position as president of the Surrey schools' cricket association is a vital link between the club and the players of the future.

The majority of our young cricketers used to come from the public schools or bigger grammar schools which offered far more opportunities for playing the game than the secondary moderns or, more recently, the comprehensives. But in Surrey we have established coaching courses and grading systems for schoolboys from the age of 12, giving many youngsters the kind of cricket tuition and practice facilities they have never had before. In this way, one would hope – indeed expect – to produce a number of good cricketers for Surrey in the next decade.

Not so long ago, there was not a great deal of incentive for a young man to make cricket his career. Indeed when I was playing it was hardly surprising that a lad would think twice about £750 a year for playing cricket when he could have gone into industry and picked up twice as much in a safe, secure job.

Nowadays, prospective cricketers can look at the likes of Bob Willis, Ian Botham and David Gower and realize that if they can reach that level, they could earn more than the Prime Minister.

5

Three Great Games

It is now close on 30 years since I had the great good
fortune to take 19 wickets for England in a Test match
again Australia, yet still scarcely a week goes by without
someone quizzing me about what actually happened at
Old Trafford in 1956.

In various publications over the years, I have offered
a few reasons for the extraordinary events of those five
memorable days. But I have never actually written about
the game, or even discussed it with anybody, in any sort
of detail. So, in response to many requests, I have finally
decided to record my thoughts and feelings before, during
and after what has inevitably come to be known as
'Laker's Match'.

It occurred to me that it might be interesting to look
back at the same time at two other Tests against Australia
which will forever be remembered for quite remarkable
individual performances, 'Jessop's Match' at the Oval in
1902 and 'Botham's Match' at Headingley in 1981. They
belong to vastly different ages. In Jessop's day, a mixture
of 'gentlemen' amateurs and 'professional' players – the
latter receiving match fees of ten pounds each – played
three-day Tests on uncovered wickets. In Botham's era,
each member of the England team was getting £1,400 a
match, plus bonuses, for five-day Tests on covered pitches
with their every need met by sponsors and their every
moment exposed by all the latest television technology.

And I found it fascinating to compare my own personal
experience with what I have heard and read of Jessop's
in the history books and what I saw of Botham's through

the medium of television in the lounge of my Putney home.

Jessop's Match

Let me start in 1902, a momentous year which saw the country still celebrating the end of the Boer War, King Edward VII, with Queen Alexandra beside him, crowned in Westminster Abbey on August 9, and, starting at the Oval two days later, one of the most dramatic games in the history of Test matches between England and Australia.

A. C. MacLaren had taken his England team to Australia the previous winter and been soundly beaten by four Tests to one, so he and the great English cricket public were thirsting for revenge when the Australians disembarked only a few weeks later. But Joe Darling and his men were equally determined to keep a tight hold on the Ashes and little was to go right for England throughout the summer.

The series began with the first Test ever to be played at Edgbaston and it looked like being a happy hunting ground for England when what is considered to be the strongest batting side they have ever assembled – all 11 had made first-class centuries – rattled up 376 for nine declared. Then Australia were skittled for just 36 with Wilfred Rhodes taking seven for 17, but after they had followed on and reached 46 for two rain prevented any further play.

Worse was to follow. At Lord's, where England had recovered from the shock of losing both C. B. Fry and Ranjitsinhji without a run on the board to reach 102 for two, rain washed out all but 105 minutes' play. And at Sheffield, in the only Test ever to be played at Bramall Lane, England were twice trapped on yet another rain-affected pitch and lost by 143 runs.

England must have felt that their luck would change at Old Trafford, but they were wrong. A superb 128 by the Hon. F. S. Jackson followed by five cheap wickets from Bill Lockwood, who accounted for Trumper, Duff, Hill and Noble for a mere 11 runs meant that England

47

needed only 123 runs to win and level the series. But, almost inevitably, the rain came down again and under very difficult conditions they failed to reach their target by just three runs in a thrilling finish.

So the series was lost, and though most people blamed the weather there was, as ever, great controversy about the selection of the England team. In those days, Test matches were organized and teams largely selected by the club where the game was staged. And at Old Trafford the local selectors had dropped Fry, Jessop, Hirst and, strangest of all, Sydney Barnes, who, even at a time when Rhodes, Hirst and Trumble were in their prime, was regarded by many as the greatest bowler of the day. He had had a triumphant winter in Australia and had taken six for 49 in the Sheffield Test, yet he was not to play for England again for more than five years.

Thankfully, George Hirst and Gilbert Jessop were both recalled for the fifth and final Test so the England team for the Oval – remember that the amateurs not only took the field by a different gate but had their titles and initials before their names on the scorecard – read:

Mr A. C. MacLaren
Mr L. C. H. Palairet
Tyldesley
Hayward
Hon. F. S. Jackson
Braund
Mr G. L. Jessop
Hirst
Lockwood
Lilley
Rhodes

The professionals were not treated extravagantly although it is fair to point out that the price of cricket bats varied between six shillings and a guinea – or 30p and £1.05p in today's money. A cricket shirt could be purchased for one and threepence (about 6p) and the best buckskin cricket boots were on sale at only eight shillings and eleven pence (about 44p). Even so, there was a lot of haggling about money.

48

A few years earlier, there had been something like a strike at the Oval when Lohmann, Gunn, Abel, Richardson and Hayward had demanded twenty pounds each as their Test match fees – or double what they had been paid in the other Tests. Surrey, who had been responsible for their selection, felt aggrieved that four of the dissidents were their own players and though they persuaded Abel, Hayward and Richardson to relent, Lohmann would not budge and was omitted from the team. The case of W. G. Grace, who made more out of cricket as an amateur than any of the professionals did, was raised and the Surrey club coyly admitted that whenever Grace played at the Oval for either the Gentlemen or for England he received ten pounds per match 'to cover expenses'.

Other amateurs were also known to have been paid and the Hon. F. S. Jackson showed real professionalism in his first Eton v. Harrow match. His father promised him a shilling for every run and a pound for every wicket, but the offer was withdrawn after the lad had scored 21 and 59 and taken 11 wickets!

The Australian team included some of the greatest names ever to represent them and they had proved themselves to be a most powerful combination in the previous two series. Most of us know, if only by repute, that most graceful of batsmen Victor Trumper, the mighty Warwick Armstrong and the guileful Hugh Trumble. But if others such as Duff, Hill and Saunders are not so well remembered, it may only be because they kept such very good company.

There was a good Oval pitch to greet the two sides on Monday 11 August and Joe Darling must have been pleased to win the toss and bat first. Trumper and Duff were the opening batsmen against the bowling of Lockwood and Rhodes – an unusual combination of pace and spin, though it was often the case in years gone by that a spinner would be given the new ball.

On this occasion, Rhodes presented few problems as Trumper and Duff took the score along to 47 and it was his great friend and Yorkshire colleague George Hirst, coming on at first change, who quickly altered the state of the game. Bowling his medium-quick, left-arm inswingers, he had Duff beautifully caught from a genuine leg glance by wicket-keeper Arthur Lilley and quickly disposed of Trumper, Hill and Darling in the space of a few overs. But Noble and Gregory stopped the rot and were still together at lunch with the score 107 for four.

After the break, Hirst soon bowled Gregory before Australia reaffirmed the depth of their batting. Noble went on to complete his 50 with support from Armstrong, Hopkins at No. 8 made 40, Kelly at No. 10 scored 39 and the formidable Trumble, batting at No. 9, was undefeated with 64. Apparently they had a share of good fortune but they rode their luck to reach a most useful 324 all out by close of play.

Then the weather, which had dogged England all summer, took a hand again. It rained heavily during the night and early morning and after an hour's play on the second day bad light held up the game for 40 minutes. The pitch, previously so good, had become treacherous and called for real caution. MacLaren took nearly an hour to score 10 runs and poor Hayward never got off the mark in his 20 minutes at the crease. Tyldesley played well but at lunch England were in dire trouble at 83 for six.

Once again it was Hirst who came to the rescue, this time with the bat, yet England still needed 38 to avoid the follow on when he was out for 43. That they did so was chiefly due to the efforts of Bill Lockwood whose 25 valuable runs saw his side through to an all-out total of 183. It also gave him and his fellow bowlers a chance to exploit a responsive wicket on which Trumble had finished with eight for 65.

Trumper immediately raised England's hopes by running himself out for only seven and suddenly Australia found that scoring runs was even more difficult for them than it had been for England. Only four of their batsmen could manage double figures and hard as they battled to survive they had scrambled only 114 for eight at the end of the second day.

On Wednesday morning, Bill Lockwood quickly snapped up the last two wickets to end with five for 45 as Australia were dismissed for 121. But the task of scoring 263 that day on a damaged and still soft pitch seemed out of the question and if there had been any bookmakers on the ground back in 1902 the odds against England doing it would have been astronomical. And such thoughts were confirmed as Saunders sent back MacLaren (2), Palairet (6), Tyldesley (0) and Hayward (7). The match looked as good as over when half the side was out for 48.

At least the Hon. F. S. Jackson was still there, and in many an innings for Yorkshire and England he had shown he was a batsman for the big occasion. Though neither as elegant as Trumper or 'Ranji' nor as majestic as MacLaren, he had unrivalled concentration and C. B. Fry said of him that he played the same game on mud as he would have played on marble.

Cricket was an interruption to a career in public service. He had just returned from two years in the army during the Boer War and he was later to give up the game to become a Member of Parliament and Governor of Bengal. While in India, he was fired at five times by a rabid Nationalist which prompted one critic to ask 'Why didn't they finish the over' and Jackson himself to remark 'The quickest duck I ever made'.

Now, as Jackson leaned on his bat, a faded Cambridge cap could be seen descending the pavilion steps. Word spread through the crowd like a ripple through a field of barley. G. L. Jessop, 'The Croucher', was on his way. England had already lost the rubber and seemed certain to lose the final Test, but here was someone who was certain to have a go.

Jessop had been bowled by Trumble for 13 in England's first innings. Indeed during the entire season he had only once made a score against these Australians who had never made a secret of their belief that he would be highly vulnerable against their bowling. But this had obviously not diminished Jessop's confidence for in the Grand Hotel the previous evening he had laid bets that he would make a century.

The bowlers were in full cry on a difficult pitch.

51

England still needed 216 to win with only five wickets left. And there were 20 minutes to play before lunch. With such thoughts in mind, most batsmen would have been full of caution and simply looking to play themselves in. But caution had never been one of Jessop's characteristics.

Tyldesley had just been bowled by the first ball of a Saunders over when Jessop arrived at the crease to take up that curious stance that gave him his nickname. The next four balls, which turned sharply into him, all went to the legside boundary despite the fact that Saunders had posted four of his fielders back on the boundary edge. And anyone who has ever played at the Oval when that huge outfield has been saturated will appreciate the immense power and superlative timing needed to pierce that sort of field placing.

To a degree, fortune favoured the brave and Jessop had a bit of luck, which was long overdue from an English viewpoint. With his score on 22, Kelly missed a stumping chance and five runs later Trumper misjudged a difficult skier at long off – which shows that Jessop was not purely concerned with legside hitting. He did not much favour the off drive but relished rattling some balls straight back into the pavilion. These shots, by the way, only produced four runs in those days. To get six, the batsman had to hit the ball clean out of the ground, and few people have ever done that at Kennington Oval!

There were five men back on the boundary after lunch when Armstrong took over from Saunders but, undeterred, Jessop took two more fours and his partnership with Jackson flourished. They had added 109 in just 65 minutes and taken the score to 157 when Jackson was caught and bowled by Trumble for 49 priceless runs.

This brought in Hirst with 106 runs still required and the Yorkshireman immediately began to strike the ball bang in the middle of the bat while Jessop continued his incredible assault on the Australian attack. The Croucher took 12 off one over from Trumble, twice hitting the ball into the pavilion, and then, with a perfectly executed late cut, reached his century. It had taken just 74 minutes –

easily the fastest hundred ever made in Test matches between England and Australia.

The crowd, which had grown to 22,000, went wild, throwing hats, scarves and handkerchiefs into the air and almost certainly breaking Jessop's concentration. For he hit just one more boundary which was not far from the reach of square leg before playing the same stroke again and giving Noble a simple catch at short leg.

So ended a quite extraordinary innings – 104 out of 139 in 77 minutes, including a 5, seventeen 4s, two 3s, four 2s and seventeen singles. But the game was still there to be won and lost. With three wickets in hand, England needed 76 to win and first Lockwood, though he made only two, and then Lilley with 16 gave Hirst real support in stands of 37 and 24. Both of them fell to Trumble, though, and 15 runs were still wanted when the last man came in. But the last man was Wilfred Rhodes.

Rhodes had been regarded purely as a bowler from his very first match – when he bowled the mighty W.G. – hence his position at the tail end of the batting order. His batting ability was discovered almost by accident when he was sent in as a night watchman and batted all through the following day. Subsequently, he was to open the batting for both Yorkshire and England, share an opening stand of 323 with Jack Hobbs and, incredibly, total 39,797 runs in his career.

It is doubtful whether any team at any time has had such a remarkable no. 11, and it was immediately apparent that Hirst had every confidence in his fellow Yorkshireman. They exchanged a few words in which, according to legend, Hirst said: 'We'll get 'em in singles'. And whether that is true or not there were nine singles among the 15 runs England needed.

Rhodes first had to see off the last ball of Trumble's over before Hirst made it clear that he had no intention of farming the bowling by taking a single off the first ball of the next over from Noble. Rhodes calmly stroked the next ball wide of slip for four before coolly playing out the remaining four deliveries.

Once again Hirst took a single off the first ball from

53

Trumble, leaving Rhodes to play out the over. And with grown men leaving the ground unable to stand the strain, the pattern continued, Hirst taking an early single in successive overs and the unruffled Rhodes standing firm.

Then a single apiece by both batsmen left England requiring just six runs to win. Two more Hirst singles, then a two (one of them an overthrow!) meant that only two were wanted as Trumble began the last over. Hirst scored the single necessary to tie the match and it was left to Rhodes to drive the ball past mid-on for the winning hit as the crowd erupted once more.

Hirst finished unbeaten on 58 and his great contribution should never be forgotten. He had taken five wickets in Australia's first innings, top scored with 43 in England's first innings and finally played in masterly fashion to ensure an England victory.

But it was probably the most amazing innings ever played that ensured that the game would always be remembered as Jessop's Match. For as Hugh Trumble was to say afterwards: 'The only man living who could beat us, beat us.'

There were two interesting postscripts. *The Times* reported that since his splendid innings at the Oval, Mr G. L. Jessop had been bothered by autograph hunters to such an extent that he had written to *The Sportsman* to say that in future he would exchange his autograph for a postal order for five shillings to be given to the Cricketers' National War Fund.

And Mr. G. H. Pardon, editor of *Wisden*, wrote: 'Given a fine day and a lively pitch, batting of the stonewalling kind is emphatically not the best of cricket and, when England and Australia meet, one would always like, irrespective of the result, to see the game at the highest level of excellence'.

AUSTRALIA

V. Trumper b Hirst	42	run out	2
R. A. Duff c Lilley b Hirst	23	b Lockwood	6
C. Hill b Hirst	11	c MacLaren b Hirst	34
J. Darling c Lilley b Hirst	3	c MacLaren b Lockwood	15
M. A. Noble c & b Jackson	52	b Braund	13
S. E. Gregory b Hirst	43	b Braund	9
W. W. Armstrong b Jackson	17	b Lockwood	21
A. Hopkins c MacLaren b Lockwood	40	c Lilley b Lockwood	3
H. Trumble not out	64	not out	7
J. J. Kelly c Rhodes b Braund	39	lbw b Lockwood	0
J. V. Saunders lbw b Braund	0	c Tyldesley b Rhodes	2
B 5, LB 3, NB 2	10	B 7, LB 2	9
	324		121

England bowling

	O	M	R	W	O	M	R	W
Lockwood	24	2	85	1	20	6	45	5
Rhodes	28	9	46	0	22	7	38	1
Hirst	29	5	77	5	5	1	7	1
Braund	16.5	5	29	2	9	1	15	2
Jackson	20	4	66	2	4	3	7	0
Jessop	6	2	11	0				

Fall of wickets

1/47 2/63 3/69 4/82 5/126
6/174 7/175 8/256 9/324 10/324

1/6 2/9 3/31 4/71 5/75
6/91 7/99 8/114 9/115 10/121

ENGLAND

Mr A. C. MacLaren c Armstrong b Trumble	10	b Saunders	2
Mr L. C. H. Palairet b Trumble	20	b Saunders	6
J. T. Tyldesley b Trumble	33	b Saunders	0
T. Hayward b Trumble	0	c Kelly b Saunders	7
Hon. F. S. Jackson c Armstrong b Saunders	2	c & b Trumble	49
L. C. Braund c Hill b Trumble	22	c Kelly b Trumble	2
Mr G. L. Jessop b Trumble	13	c Noble b Armstrong	104
G. H. Hirst c & b Trumble	43	not out	58
W. H. Lockwood c Noble b Saunders	25	lbw b Trumble	2
A. A. Lilley c Trumper b Trumble	0	c Darling b Trumble	16
W. Rhodes not out	0	not out	6
B 13, LB 2	15	B 5, LB 6	11
	183	for 9	263

Australian bowling

	O	M	R	W	O	M	R	W
Trumble	31	13	65	8	33.5	4	108	4
Saunders	23	7	79	2	24	3	105	4
Noble	7	3	24	0	5	0	11	0
Armstrong					4	0	28	1

Fall of wickets

1/31 2/36 3/62 4/67 5/67 6/83
7/137 8/179 9/183 10/183

1/5 2/5 3/10 4/31 5/48
6/157 7/187 8/214 9/248

Laker's Match

I had plenty to occupy my mind during the leisurely, six-hour drive in my battered Austin Somerset from our small flat in West Hampstead up the old A6 to Manchester. The date was 25 July 1956, just eight days after England had beaten Australia by an innings and 42 runs in the third Test at Headingley to level the Ashes series.

My Surrey colleague Tony Lock and I had shared 18 of the 20 Australian wickets – and had bowled 137 overs between us – and were more than pleased that the county was without a major fixture over the next three days. I had not expected to miss the match which followed this respite since it was sure to be vital in the battle for the County Championship. It was back in Yorkshire, at Bramall Lane, Sheffield, and Willie Watson had shrewdly chosen it as his benefit game. But Surrey, in their wisdom as it turned out, decided to give me a further three days' rest because my spinning finger was showing a certain amount of wear and tear.

The Yorkshire match turned out to be a low-scoring affair which produced a nail-biting finish. Yorkshire, needing only 97 to win, began the last day at 30 for two. Then the remarkable G.A.R. Lock went to work and in 11 overs took five wickets for 11 so that Surrey scrambled home by 14 runs. This meant that in the three games prior to the fourth Test Lock had taken 29 wickets – including all ten in one innings against Kent at Blackheath – at a cost of 7.4 runs apiece and was hardly short of form or lacking in confidence as he and captain Peter May made their way over the Pennines to report to Old Trafford.

I was thinking about that on my lonely journey north, and reflecting on the fact that Old Trafford had never been a happy hunting ground for me. In 1948, against Australia, I had been omitted from the twelve on the morning of the match. And the same thing happened against New Zealand the following year when I was left out in favour of the Yorkshire prodigy, Brian Close, who became the youngest cricketer ever to play for England at the age of 18 years 149 days.

56

My first Test at Manchester, against the West Indies in 1950, turned out to be a disaster. My one wicket cost 86 runs and I was dropped for the rest of the series. I did better in 1951, taking four for 89 against South Africa which remained my best match figures in an Old Trafford Test.

I was given only two overs there in 1952 when the Indians were annihilated by Fred Trueman. And though I returned to take three for 53 against Australia in 1953, I did not even make the squad against Pakistan in 1954 or South Africa in 1955 when Jim McConnon and Fred Titmus respectively were the off-spinners.

My record, then, in six previous Test-match visits to Old Trafford added up to a paltry eight wickets at a cost of 29 each. My performances for Surrey against Lanca-shire there had scarcely been better. And I came to the conclusion that with Locky in such great form there was every chance of a reversal of our roles at Leeds where I had taken 11 wickets to Tony's seven – always assuming that I was in the side.

I need not have worried. It was a season in which the selectors, for once, could do no wrong. They had already recalled one of their colleagues, Cyril Washbrook, at the age of 41 for the Leeds Test and he had gone in at 17 for three, scored 98 and shared a partnership of 187 with Peter May which proved to be the turning point in the series. Now they had gambled again by recalling the Rev. David Sheppard despite the fact that he had had only two or three recent games behind him. They had also added Tom Graveney to the squad, but he damaged a hand in practice and Alan Oakman, who had made his debut at Leeds, was reinstated at the last minute.

When everything had been sorted out, the England side showed two changes from the successful Leeds XI, Sheppard replacing Doug Insole and Brian Statham taking over from Fred Trueman, much to the Yorkshire-man's disgust. Fred has told me many times over the years: 'Tha would never 'ave got 19 wickets if I'd been laikin'!' And I must admit that it is still hard to believe that either Trueman or Statham could possibly have been omitted.

Both of them were simply magnificent fast bowlers and I have always found it impossible to decide who was the better, Fred with his classical action and wonderful late away-swinger or Brian of equal pace and accuracy personified with a really vicious break-back. But the selectors, walking on water as they were until the final Test at the Oval when they reinstated Denis Compton after his knee operation and he delighted everyone with 94 typical runs, opted for a four-man attack. And for Old Trafford it was going to be Statham, Bailey, Laker and Lock with Oakman's off-breaks in support.

Australia, meanwhile, were able to choose from all 17 members of their touring party for the first time in the series. They dropped Peter Burge to give 19-year-old Ian Craig his first Test against England. Gil Langley was scheduled to return behind the stumps but, bizarre as it may sound, he fell asleep on his hand the night before the match and damaged it sufficiently to put himself out of the reckoning. But even with Len Maddocks continuing to deputize for Langley, their final line-up looked a truly formidable one.

The team was drawn from just three states – four Victorians, four New South Welshmen and three Queenslanders – which seems inconceivable today after what South Australia and, especially, Western Australia have achieved in recent years. All 11 had made centuries in first-class cricket and eight of them in Test matches. And the old firm of Lindwall and Miller was supported by the promising Archer and spinners Benaud and Johnson.

For me at that stage of the season, net practice was of the gentlest kind, even on the eve of a Test match. Normally towards the end of July, I had already bowled something like 1,000 overs and, in any case, I had no wish to aggravate my spinning finger. I contented myself with a few exercises to remove the stiffness of the long car ride before taking a stroll out to the wicket.

I have never placed too much importance on the ritual of inspecting a pitch the day before a match. It may well look green and grassy only to change completely after a final cut. But even from a distance the pitch at Old Trafford that day was clearly not grassy. As I drew closer, I met the great man himself, Sir Don Bradman, on his way back to the pavilion.

'How is it?' I asked.

'It's flat and slow', he replied, 'with plenty of runs in it.'

I studied that pitch much longer than I usually did, having quickly decided that for once in a while I was pleased that I was not earning my living as a fast bowler. The Don was right. It was flat and slow and would be very short of pace, and though there was not likely to be a shortage of runs, they would be harder to come by as the game progressed. Back in the dressing room, Peter May asked for my opinion.

'There is a big bonus for the side that bats first,' I told him. 'Win the toss and we shall retain the Ashes.'

England duly won the toss and made 459, which is a point that often seems to have been overlooked in the great controversy that has raged over that Old Trafford pitch for almost 30 years, especially in Australia where some people are still going on about it. They often accuse English players of being 'whinging Poms' in Australia, so where does that leave someone like their former captain, Bobby Simpson?

Simpson has gone on record as saying that the Old Trafford pitch in 1956 was unfair, though I have no recollection of his being anywhere near Manchester at the time. And what does he mean by 'unfair'? Unfair to whom? I have a sneaking feeling that some of the England bowlers must have felt that the same Old Trafford pitch was unfair in 1964 when the same R. B. Simpson bored the pants off the Lancashire crowd by batting twelve-and-threequarter hours for 311. On that occasion, England's two off-spinners, Titmus and Mortimore, finished up with combined figures of nought for 222.

It also irritates me that while it appears to be quite acceptable for the quicker bowlers to be able to whistle the ball around a batsman's ears or move the ball three or four inches off the pitch at 70 m.p.h., there is an outcry if the poor old spinner manages to turn it a few inches on the first day of a Test. Not that that happened at Old Trafford anyway. Ian Johnson, recently described by Bill O'Reilly, no less, as one of the best Australian spinners, took four for 151, while Richie Benaud, arguably the best of all Australian leg-spinners, took two for 123. So it was hardly a spinner's paradise.

Indeed the England openers, Peter Richardson and Colin Cowdrey, took such advantage of the docile track that their opening stand of 174 was made at only slightly under a run a minute. Peter's 104 was his first Test century and has been the cause of much leg-pulling ever since. We have been together at innumerable functions where the conversation has got around to Manchester 1956 and I have turned to Peter and asked him if he played in that game! It was probably one of his finest innings yet we firmly believe that only about one in 50 people were aware of his performance.

There was rather more recognition for the Rev. D. S. Sheppard who went in at number three and top scored with 113. He was one of five amateurs occupying the first five positions in our batting order – something which had last happened against Australia back in 1899 and was never to be repeated again. In many ways, Sheppard looked much more like a professional at the crease than Richardson, Cowdrey or May ever did. Indeed Cyril Coote, a much-loved figure at Fenners for so many years, always maintained that the cricketing bishop was the greatest university batsman of his time. I find that hard to swallow because I doubt if he ever had the flair of either Cowdrey or May, but he was more of a grafter and worked enormously hard at his game.

On this occasion he occupied the crease for just on five hours for his 113 – the kind of scoring rate for which Geoffrey Boycott has since been castigated! – but England had reached their all-out total of 459 in just 492 minutes which was pretty rapid progress in Test match terms.

It was only half past two on the second day when Colin McDonald and Jimmy Burke began Australia's reply.

They were both highly regarded by all the England team. I always looked upon McDonald as a typical Aussie. He was a tough, relentless opening batsman who had never been known to sell his wicket cheaply and loved the atmosphere of an England–Australia series. His speciality was the now old-fashioned cut and no one has ever played it better than he did. In fact he perfected it to such a degree that he seemed to be able to put half-volleys away wide of gully. As for Burke he was solid and the more orthodox of the two, but I fancied I had a better chance of getting him out because the impression was always there of a slight gap between bat and pad when he was pushing forward on the off side.

The first 10 overs, bowled by Statham and Bailey, were uneventful and cost just 10 runs before Peter May turned to his spin attack with Lock operating at the Stretford End and myself at the Warwick Road End. There were still no alarms for an over or two and I was grateful when it was decided we should switch ends. I had always favoured the Stretford End, though to this day I have no idea why.

Then, with the score on 48, I made the breakthrough, thanks to Lock who snapped up one of the 830 catches he took during his career and sent McDonald on his way for 32. The very next ball, I have always believed, went a long way towards retaining the Ashes.

Neil Harvey was the finest left-hander I ever bowled against and in our many challenging duels in the past the honours had gone very much his way. But as luck would have it this time, I managed to bowl him a beauty first ball. From around the wicket, I held it back sufficiently for the ball to drift in and pitch around leg and middle stump on a perfect length before it turned just enough to clip the off stump. Sadly the cameras could not have been rolling at that precise moment since that wicket is not included in the now familiar film, yet it was the one I treasured most.

Looking up to the Australian balcony, one could already sense a certain amount of panic in the camp – and what followed proved it. Craig stopped the hat-trick

61

but at 62 Lock took his solitary wicket when Burke was neatly taken by Cowdrey at slip. Then, without any addition to the score, Craig went back instead of forward to be lbw, poor Kenny Mackay was caught by Oakman at slip and five wickets were down for 62.

I suppose it is not very often that an Englishman holds much sympathy for an Australian, especially in the middle of a tensely fought Test series. But I genuinely felt sorry for Mackay that summer. He was an exceptionally fine player yet when the ball turned at Leeds and Manchester he looked like a complete novice and made only four runs in four innings. It was hard to believe it was the same Mackay who had roasted the great Lindwall in his prime and was still to average 125 in a series in South Africa; the same Mackay who became the first Australian to play in more than 100 Sheffield Shield matches and was respected wherever he played; the same Mackay who is now so sadly missed in his beloved Queensland.

With McDonald, Harvey, Burke, Craig and Mackay back in the pavilion, Australia were now looking to Keith Miller, their most experienced batsman, to salvage the innings. But he was in no sort of form and when Oakman took his second catch, Keith departed in great haste as usual, leaving his side tottering at 73 for six.

So it was all down to Ron Archer and Richie Benaud, both handsome strikers of a cricket ball and at 22 and 25 respectively already earmarked as the two players most likely to lead Australia back to their position as the best team in the world. Everyone knows how well Richie succeeded in reaching the top in every facet of the game. But I wonder how many people realize what a tragedy it was for Australian cricket when Ron's Test career came to an abrupt end in 1956 because of a serious knee injury which totally incapacitated him. I am certain he would have made an indelible mark on world cricket with his aggressive batting and new-ball bowling.

It was characteristic of them both that they decided to try to launch an attack on me but Archer was brilliantly stumped by Godfrey Evans for only six and Benaud only succeeded in finding the very safe hands of Statham at long on before he had scored. Maddocks and Johnson were both clean bowled in rapid succession and Australia were all out for 84. To my utter amazement, I had picked up seven wickets for eight runs in just 22 balls after tea and finished the innings with nine for 37.

Naturally the pitch was the subject of further discussion during the break prior to the follow-on. There was no doubt that anyone who really spun the ball as opposed to rolling it off the fingers would get appreciable turn but at no time in the previous two hours had it turned at any great speed and there was certainly no lift or bounce whatsoever. After all, Tony Lock had by no means bowled badly yet had taken only one wicket for 37. And the general opinion was that a good county side would have been disappointed to have made less than 200 to 250 while any spinner would happily have settled for something like five for 60.

I still believe we had witnessed one of the worst exhibitions of batting ever by an Australian side. There is no doubt that they panicked, believing the wicket was far worse than it really was. Batting techniques were quite deplorable with the main fault being that batsmen were pushing forward defensively much too hard at the ball. They were therefore making contact with a spinning delivery with the bat too often more than a foot ahead of the pad, thereby accelerating the ball towards the close catchers. It is a fault that you rarely see among present-day batsmen.

Australia were unfortunate when they followed on in that McDonald had to retire hurt with a knee injury after scoring 11 of the 28 runs on the board. And they were even more unfortunate when Harvey came and went for the only 'king pair' of his illustrious career.

We obviously needed to put the pressure on to try to prevent him from sneaking a quick single and I noticed that Cowdrey was slightly too deep at mid-on. I asked Colin to move closer in but I did not realize as I moved in to bowl that he had crept several yards further than I wanted.

In the first innings, I had bowled Harvey with my best ball of the summer. Now I let him have what was by far the worst ball sent down in the entire match, a slow, gentle full toss on the leg stump which must have looked as if I was giving him one off the mark. Neil, obviously caught in two minds as to whether to hit it for four or six, stopped his shot and finished up by pushing it tamely into the hands of Cowdrey, who by then was in no man's land somewhere between mid-on and forward short leg. No wonder Harvey tossed his bat high in the air in exasperation before departing for the pavilion.

That was the final disaster to befall Australia on that eventful second day as the solid Burke and the youthful Craig played soundly through to the close when they had reached 51 for one. And I was in a particular hurry to leave the ground because my wife, Lilly, was travelling up by train to watch Saturday's play and I was to meet her at Warrington Station.

Hailing from the lovely city of Vienna, Lilly was not a keen student of the game but she very much enjoyed her days out at Test matches in the fifties, none more so than when it meant a couple of days away from home at Leeds or Manchester. She was quite unprepared, though, for the scene that greeted her at Warrington. The poor girl had not seen a paper or listened to the radio and was quite unaware of the fact that I had taken 10 wickets to date, or that I would be escorted to the platform by a host of Press reporters together with their photographers.

'Good Lord!' she said. 'What on earth have you been up to?'

And I had to explain to her what I had been doing all day before we could pose for the cameras.

Her arrival coincided with a dramatic change in the weather. As a result, there was only 45 minutes' play on the Saturday when only six runs were scored for the loss of Burke's wicket, yet another victim of the 'caught Lock bowled Laker' combination.

Sunday was another atrocious day. It was as dark and wet as November and we were grateful for the warm hospitality of our host, the late Roger Allen, at the

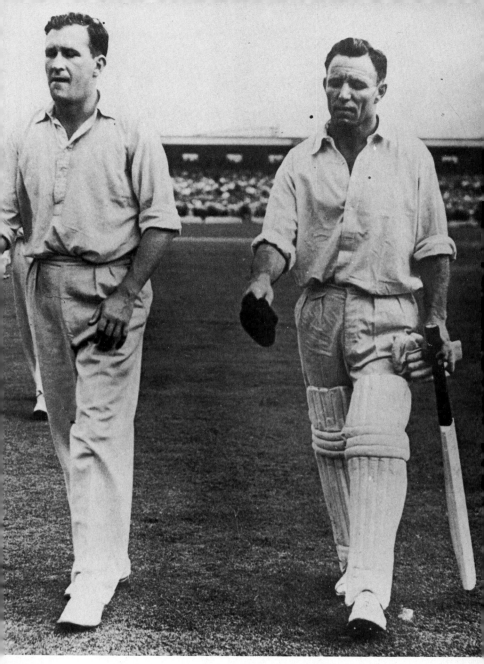

Returning to the pavilion with Ray Lindwall at the end of Australia's first innings at Old Trafford in 1956 when I took 19 wickets in the match. Ray had remained not out – but he was not so lucky in the second innings

Yorkshiremen will probably argue for ever about who was the greater of these two opening batsmen, but Sir Leonard Hutton will always be my No 1. All the concentration and determination behind Geoffrey Boycott's famous defensive technique is captured here, but Leonard had a wider range of scoring strokes including this perfectly executed cut

Freddie Trueman's classical, sideways-on fast bowler's action contrasts vividly with the ungainly, open-chested style of Bob Willis. But both of them were highly effective with their differing methods, as their Test records – Willis 325 wickets, Trueman 307 – proved

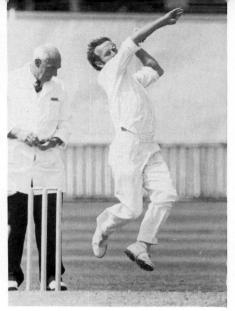

Above: Slow, left-arm spinners! The sheer, unbridled aggression of Tony Lock (*left*) is caught dramatically in this superb action photograph of my old Surrey sparring partner, but the look in Derek Underwood's (*right*) eyes shows there is no less determination as he settles into the perfectly balanced, rhythmic action that made him the most accurate of all bowlers

Below: Keith Miller (*right*) shows the flamboyant style that made him one of the greatest crowd-pleasers of his day, but I don't think he ever hit the ball quite as hard as Ian Botham (*left*) whose awesome power is demonstrated in this perfect example of the straight six

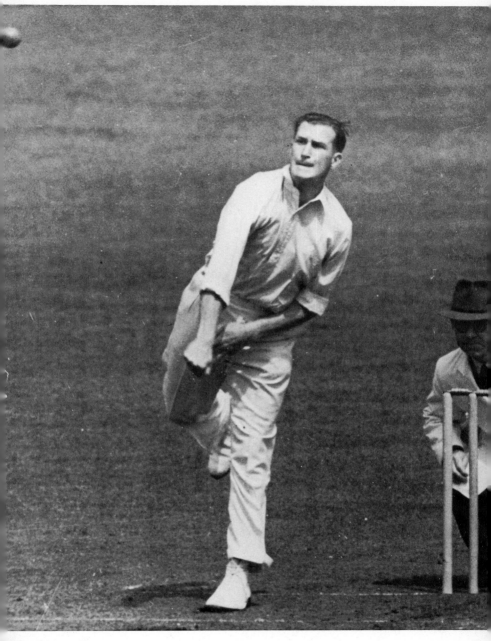

hn Emburey (*left*), who I consider to be the best off-spin bowler in the game today, shows a rtain similarity in his action with my own action, but with one obvious and basic difference he delivery stride. I always believed the shorter stride allowed for more variation in flight … it I'm thankful we played in different eras!

Perfect balance by both Peter May (*right*), England's finest post-war batsman, and the left-handed David Gower (*above*) who still has some way to go to surpass him. No one ever played the on-drive better than P. B. H. – though on a good day Gower can make every shot in the book look so easy

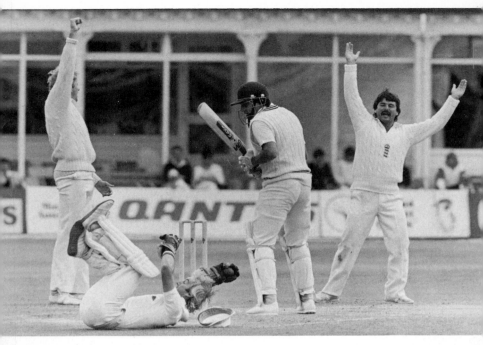

Two of the greatest wicket-keepers of all time. Godfrey Evans (*below*), lively and effervescent, and Bob Taylor (*above*), quiet and studious, are so very different off the field but on it they could both be super showmen. Here, Godfrey makes a typical stumping while Taylor, as agi as ever at the age of 42, takes a spectacular catch

delightful Lymm Hotel where the England team used to stay in those days. By early evening, I was back at Warrington Station to put Lilly on the train back to London – though if we had known what was going to happen during the next two days she would certainly have stayed on to share in the greatest moment of my career. It is something we have both regretted to this day.

Not that she would have had much to celebrate on the Monday. The weather was still horrible. It had stopped raining at last but the pitch – left uncovered, of course – was saturated and to make matters worse gale force winds had sprung up to make both batting and bowling extremely difficult.

Ordinary bails were useless and were replaced by some made of the much heavier lignum, which proved very effective. In fact they were never disturbed in just two spells of cricket which allowed only an hour's play. The wet pitch was quite dead and Craig and the gallant McDonald, who had returned to the crease, were never in trouble as the score moved on to 84 for two.

Happily for England if not Australia, Tuesday 31 July dawned fine and dry. The clouds were high and play began only ten minutes late with Australia needing another 291 runs with eight wickets in hand to avoid an innings defeat. The wicket was soaked, slow and very easy paced, giving no spin at all, and Craig and McDonald were still not unduly worried in playing through the morning session and taking the score along to 112 for two. As we went in to lunch, the odds seemed to favour Australia hanging on for a draw.

I did not join the team for lunch but settled for putting my feet up with a beer and a sandwich in the dressing room. And as I gazed out towards the Derbyshire hills, the clouds began to disappear and the sun burst through. It was as though someone's prayers were being answered for an hour of sunshine would obviously bring another dramatic change in the conditions – and, of course, the match.

That is precisely what happened. Craig's tough and courageous display, which lasted four hours 20 minutes and produced 38 runs, ended when he was lbw for the second time in the match and in nine overs Mackay, Miller and Archer all went without scoring. I had taken four more wickets for just three runs and with the sun continuing to beat down found myself in a situation that spin bowlers usually only dream about.

The wicket was at its most vicious after tea and the best innings of the match was over when McDonald was caught at short leg by Oakman for 89. Colin had held us at bay for five hours 37 minutes without giving a chance in what was probably the best innings ever played by an Australian on a turning pitch in England. By then, the poor old Aussies, who had already accused Lancashire of preparing the pitch specially for the England spinners, must have felt that the arrangements were now in the hands of an even higher authority, though Richie Benaud, a good friend and colleague for many years now, defended with great skill and judgement for close on two hours before becoming my eighth victim.

I must have been asked a thousand times about my feelings at that particular moment. What pressures was I under as I realized that the record was within my grasp? Strangely enough, I felt completely relaxed. Odd as it may seem now, I did not even consider the possibilities of taking all 10 wickets. In any case, how could I when Tony Lock at the other end was fizzing the ball through against numbers nine, ten and jack with venomous lift and spin.

Many people have propounded the theory that 'dear old Locky' must have been looking to give me the last two wickets, but having known him for nearly 40 years I can assure them that that could never have been the case. Such a course of action would never even have crossed his mind. And, anyway, why should it have done? I certainly did not want him to do anything that would devalue my own performance.

In fact Lock made three highly optimistic appeals for lbw with balls missing by a couple of feet before taking yet another catch that enabled me to dispose of Lindwall. The end came quickly when Maddocks, back on his stumps, was palpably lbw. At twenty minutes past five on the final day, the demoralized Australians had been beaten by an innings and 170 runs and the Ashes had been retained.

There were no leaps in the air, no embraces, no punching the sky, just a dozen polite handshakes as I slung my sweater over one shoulder and jogged quietly up the pavilion steps.

I have never been a demonstrative person and have always tried to take whatever success has come my way just the same as I have accepted the innumerable failures. In moments of triumph, one was credited with being modest and possibly a little shy. The problem was that when one adopted the same attitude in walking off the field with nought for 100, it left one open to allegations of disinterest and even, on one memorable occasion, of not trying. Nothing could ever have been further from the truth.

The post-mortem on the game naturally centred on the state of the pitch. You know my thoughts about that. Suffice it to say that it was only during the last two or three hours that it became really difficult. The most remarkable features of the game were undoubtedly the comparative bowling figures of Tony Lock and myself. Just look at them:–

	Overs	Maidens	Runs	Wickets
Laker	68	27	90	19
Lock	69	33	106	1

If my performance was unbelievable, then so was his, for if the game had been replayed a million times it would surely never have happened again. Early on, he bowled beautifully without any luck at all and beat the bat and stumps time after time. But as wickets tumbled at the other end desperation began to creep in and he bowled faster and faster and consequently shorter and shorter.

On reflection over many years now – and remembering that he has had to live with his one for 106 – I think I should probably have shown a bit more sympathy towards him than I did at the time. I have often tried to imagine how I would have felt if the boot had been on the other foot – as it so easily could have been.

The final blow for my old mate came as we sat together in the dressing room afterwards. Brylcreem made an annual award for the best bowling performance of the season – a silver cup plus £100, which was real money in those days. My ten for 88 for Surrey against the Australians led the field until Ken Smales, another Yorkshire-born off-spinner who became secretary of Nottingham Forest, took all ten wickets for 66 for Nottinghamshire against Gloucestershire at Stroud. Everyone thought that would settle it because it was most unusual for two bowlers to take ten in the same season. But early in July Surrey played Kent on a wet wicket at Blackheath and with me on the sidelines through injury Tony had a great match, picking up 16 wickets, including 10 for 54 in the second innings. So there we were at Old Trafford waiting for Peter May to come in with the bowling figures . . . and when he revealed that my 10 for 53 had pipped poor old Tony by a single run and robbed him of £100, it really must have been the last straw.

Money has never been my god but it is interesting to look at that aspect in view of the fact that countless people have told me what my 19 wickets would have earned for me if I had performed the feat in the eighties – there is no doubt that I would have been financially secure for the rest of my days. It was rather different in 1956. For a start there was my Test match fee of £75, though that was reduced by £15 for missing two Surrey games. Then there were two cheques from Littlewoods Pools and Barclays Bank for £250 each, and De La Rue Ltd., for whom I had previously done some work, kindly contributed £10 for each wicket. Three short articles for a national daily newspaper brought in another £150 but to show how commercially naïve we were in those days I signed 1,000 copies of the final scorecard which sold like hot cakes for my benefit – at two shillings each.

I suppose I must have netted an extra £1,000 in total. But I attached far greater value to the two match balls, suitably inscribed, and a truly magnificent silver salver from the MCC, which was presented to me by Field Marshall, Earl Alexander of Tunis. Not to be outdone, his great partner, Lord Montgomery of Alamein, forwarded an autographed £1 note. They are still treasured possessions.

It was getting on for eight o'clock by the time television, radio, the Press and many well-wishers finished with me at Old Trafford and I finally pulled out of the car park to begin the long drive back to London, which I had to make for the very good reason that Surrey were playing the Australians at the Oval the following day.

I had been going for about two hours when I began to feel hungry and thirsty and decided to pull into a pub at Lichfield. Inside the crowded bar, a tiny black and white television set was showing the highlights of the last day's play in the Test match. But not a single person recognized me as I perched at the end of the bar, sipping a beer, munching away at a couple of very stale cheese sandwiches – and listening in fascination to the comments of the other customers.

If I thought that that was the end of all the fuss, however, I was sadly mistaken. There were yet more Pressmen and photographers lying in wait for me as I drew up to our flat in NW6 at two o'clock in the morning. And it was not long before my two little girls, Fiona and Angela, then aged four and two and fast asleep, had been hauled out of bed to face the cameras. But what could one say? These fellows have a living to earn. And I suppose I wished the day would never end.

At the most, I managed a couple of hours' sleep before checking in, bleary-eyed and weary, at the Oval around 10.15 a.m. But the gods were still with me. It poured with rain all morning and play was abandoned for the day.

CRICKET CONTRASTS

ENGLAND

P. E. Richardson c Maddocks b Benaud	104
M. C. Cowdrey c Maddocks b Lindwall	80
Rev. D. S. Sheppard b Archer	113
P. B. H. May c Archer b Benaud	43
T. E. Bailey b Johnson	20
C. Washbrook lbw b Johnson	6
A. S. M. Oakman c Archer b Johnson	10
T. G. Evans st Maddocks b Johnson	47
J. C. Laker run out	3
G. A. R. Lock not out	25
J. B. Statham c Maddocks b Lindwall	0
B 2, LB 5, w 1	8
	459

Australian bowling

	O	M	R	W
Lindwall	21.3	6	63	2
Miller	21	6	41	0
Archer	22	6	73	1
Johnson	47	10	151	4
Benaud	47	17	123	2

Fall of wickets

1/174 2/195 3/288 4/321 5/327 6/339 7/401 8/417 9/458 10/459

AUSTRALIA

C. C. McDonald c Lock b Laker	32	c Oakman b Laker	89
J. W. Burke c Cowdrey b Lock	22	c Lock b Laker	33
R. N. Harvey b Laker	0	c Cowdrey b Laker	0
I. D. Craig lbw b Laker	8	lbw b Laker	38
K. R. Miller c Oakman b Laker	6	b Laker	0
K. Mackay c Oakman b Laker	0	c Oakman b Laker	0
R. G. Archer st Evans b Laker	6	c Oakman b Laker	0
R. Benaud c Statham b Laker	0	b Laker	18
R. R, Lindwall not out	6	c Lock b Laker	8
L. Maddocks b Laker	4	lbw b Laker	2
I. W. Johnson b Laker	0	not out	1
		B 12, LB 4	16
	84		205

England Bowling

	O	M	R	W	O	M	R	W
Statham	6	3	6	0	16	9	15	0
Bailey	4	3	4	0	20	8	31	0
Laker	16.4	4	37	9	51.2	23	53	10
Lock	14	3	37	1	55	30	69	0
Oakman					8	3	21	0

Fall of wickets

1/48 2/48 3/62 4/62 5/62
6/73 7/73 8/74 9/84 10/84

1/28 2/55 3/114 4/124 5/130
6/130 7/181 8/198 9/203 10/205

Umpires: F. S. Lee and E. Davies.

Botham's Match

When Ian Botham finally finds the time to sit back and reflect on a truly remarkable sporting career, the year of 1981 will figure most prominently in his thoughts. Nor will Mike Brearley or Bob Willis ever wish to forget it. For me, though, it is a year that I would willingly erase for ever from my memory.

I suppose I had been extremely fortunate to have survived the previous 59 years without ever having to spend more than a couple of days in bed through illness. My attendance at a hospital had been purely in a visiting capacity and for years I had been the ideal client for BUPA or PPP. Then, suddenly, on the eve of my departure to Barbados on 10 March to catch up with the England tour of the West Indies, I was laid low with severe pains and a high temperature. The following day I was taken by ambulance to my local hospital, subjected to a series of tests which apparently diagnosed a virus infection and sent back home. Three days later, with my temperature back to normal but feeling decidedly weak and wobbly, I pronounced myself fit to leave for the Caribbean on 15 March.

The telephone rang just as we were about to leave for Heathrow and I was given the shattering news that my good friend and former Surrey colleague, Ken Barrington, had died in Barbados a few hours earlier. I had nurtured him as a 16-year-old and I liked to believe that in some small way I had been of assistance as he matured into England's most dependable post-war batsman. Now, at 50, he was gone and the whole cricket world was grief-stricken. And my visit to the West Indies became a nightmare as I drifted around Barbados and Antigua like a zombie. I was more than relieved when the time came to return to London.

For a good six weeks after that, all seemed to be going well and I felt much more like a human being again – until the Surrey Old Players' Dinner on 13 May. All of a sudden, the fever and the pains were back and I left my guests stranded at the Oval to beat a hasty retreat back home.

71

My wife Lilly, in her wisdom, acted swiftly and Lance Bromley, a good friend and leading surgeon at St. Mary's Hospital, Paddington, was quickly at my bedside. His prompt and accurate diagnosis unquestionably saved my life. Almost immediately, I was rushed into hospital and on 15 May I underwent a five-hour operation for an aortic aneurism. Lance had persuaded Mr Eastcott, a top surgeon specializing in diseases of the main artery, to perform the operation and I could not have been in better hands. I had no idea how seriously ill I had become and it was only later, when I came out of intensive care, that I learned what a close call it had been. Letters arrived by the hundred and, as the days went by, visitors by the score. As June came in, I was back home again but progress was slow. I was in bed for the best part of a month and when I eventually got up, a walk to the end of the road and back seemed like the London Marathon.

Meanwhile a momentous cricket season was under way, and for the first time in more than ten years I was to miss being in my usual Test match commentary position. My sanity was saved by BBC television. It is on such occasions that one can really appreciate what television means to the aged, the sick and infirm, the poor and the incapacitated. I was glued to my set for two solid months and never missed a ball.

Australia had sent a very useful-looking side under the captaincy of Kim Hughes although they were obviously going to miss Greg Chappell who had decided it was time to take a break from Test cricket. They had gambled on the promise of Terry Alderman, an uncapped medium-quick bowler from Perth, Western Australia, who was to form a very formidable new-ball partnership with the great Dennis Lillee and prove the success story of the tour.

Despite a good deal of controversy after the loss of two successive Test series against the mighty West Indies, England decided to retain Ian Botham as captain. I had felt all along that it was a mistake to saddle such a magnificent all-rounder with the added problems of captaincy. He had by no means been a failure as a captain but there was always the worrying thought that it would affect his own performance and we needed him at his brilliant best to beat Australia. My considered opinion was that it would be no great surprise if he came back to skipper England with success in the future but for the time being it would be far better to see someone else spinning the coin.

As it happened, Botham lost the toss in the first Test at Trent Bridge, Hughes put England in to bat and Australia went on to win by a margin of four wickets inside four days with Trevor Chappell, the youngest of the three brothers, making the winning hit on his debut. Botham, who made only a single in the first innings before becoming one of Alderman's nine victims in the match, top-scored with 33 second time round but took only three of the 16 Australian wickets to fall.

Two weeks later at Lord's, Ian lost the toss again and though the game ended in a draw his fortunes with the bat also reached rock bottom. For the first time in his Test career, he was dismissed in both innings without scoring and he looked down and dejected as he made his way back to the pavilion on a walk which must have seemed interminable. Before the game was over, he had a long discussion with Alec Bedser, chairman of the selectors, and soon afterwards it was announced that there would be a change of captaincy for the third Test. The next morning it was announced that Mike Brearley was returning to lead the side.

For Botham it was back to Somerset for a three-day championship game against Sussex, and whether or not it felt as though a huge weight had been removed from those broad shoulders it certainly looked that way as he walked out in front of his own fanatical Taunton supporters and hammered the Sussex attack for 72 in just 17 overs. It was just the sort of net he needed before the long drive up to Leeds.

England had made two changes for what was clearly a very vital Test match. Bob Woolmer was the batsman who had to stand down to make way for Brearley and, to the delight of the locals, Chris Old was recalled in place of John Emburey. Thus our attack consisted of four pace bowlers plus Peter Willey as a makeshift spinner – a balance which Brearley later admitted caused him to lose a bit of sleep on the first night.

Kim Hughes, with an unchanged side, won the toss yet again but he, too, must have harboured a few doubts about his decision to bat first this time on a grey, overcast morning. And he was indebted to John Dyson, who made a sound and solid 102, when Australia ended a shortened first day at 203 for three, while Brearley was not overjoyed at the sight of three reasonable chances being spilled.

The second day was both pedestrian and wearisome, to say the least. Hughes went on to make 89 and Graham Yallop weighed in with 58 valuable runs. Not for the first time, it was left to Botham to salvage some English pride by finishing with six for 95, though the combined figures of Willis and Old – nought for 163 – hardly did them justice. Hughes's declaration at 401 for nine allowed Lillee and Alderman an over apiece against Geoff Boycott and Graham Gooch which they survived without mishap.

It was not what you would call enthralling viewing. Indeed with England achieving an over rate of only 15 overs per hour for the best part of two days the cricket had been dull and boring in the extreme, and if anyone had suggested that we were on the threshold of one of the most gripping games in Test history I for one would not have believed it.

Yet, for me, it was a fascinating experience to sit – or occasionally lie – in front of a television set all day long, which was something I had not done since the days when Brian Johnston and Peter West were doing ball-by-ball commentaries and Denis Compton was giving an expert opinion. Above all, it gave me the opportunity to appreciate more than ever what an outstanding contribution Richie Benaud has made to BBC television in recent years. The principal criticism of Richie in this country has never had anything to do with the quality of his cricket commentary but has simply been due to the fact that he was born an Australian. Some people, including eminent members of the MCC, believe that the

BBC should not employ an Australian to comment full time on Test matches in which Australia are not involved. It is strange that some of the same people have been responsible for flooding English cricket with overseas players! On top of that, of course, Richie has not been easily forgiven his association with a certain Mr Kerry Packer, which caused so much embarrassment at Lord's.

Packer's Channel Nine in Australia now looms large as a serious rival to the BBC, who were the pioneers of cricket coverage world-wide. But that is mainly due to the vast amount of money that has been made available for production costs whereas the BBC have been compelled to work on a much more limited budget. It should not be forgotten, either, that ten years ago Australian cricket coverage was pretty puerile, to say the least. And their technical improvement has owed a great deal to the visits of two BBC producers, the late David Kenning and Nick Hunter.

The biggest problem facing the cricket commentators – at least those who fully understand the game – is in deciding how much talk is necessary to satisfy the demands of an extremely mixed audience. One always has to be aware that among the viewers there are those with a deep understanding of the game yet others who are completely bemused by such expressions as 'late inswing' or 'movement off the seam'; those with a great knowledge of its history who may still be living in the days of Hobbs and Larwood, yet others who believe that Woolley is a kind of cricket sweater; and again there are those who sit in front of the 'box' throughout the day while others watch for just the odd half-hour. Constant repetition can irritate the former but the latter would be frustrated if they were not made aware of all the facts.

Added to all those considerations are other complications for the commentator, such as the situation that can occur when BBC 2 is covering the last hour's play on a Saturday afternoon. All is peaceful and serene when suddenly BBC 1, getting towards the end of their afternoon sports transmission, come in for a 45-second summary of the day's play. BBC 2 viewers, unaware of what is happening, must often think we have all gone raving mad. And no sooner have they got over that than 'Look North' will arrive for a similar exercise. . . .

I sat at home and watched all these goings-on with a wry smile, while back at Headingley England and their supporters had nothing to smile about at all. The third day's play proved disastrous with England dismissed for 174 as Alderman, Lillee and Geoff Lawson gave them an object lesson in bowling on a pitch giving help to the seamers. This was most unusual because for years English bowlers have shown a marked superiority over all others under such conditions. Often in the past the Australians had bowled too short, but the reverse happened this time. They bowled a much better line and a fuller length with the result that wickets fell steadily. Again, only Botham made any sort of impact. Without any captaincy worries to encumber him, he cracked a rapid 50 to add to his six wickets.

Brearley certainly had his worries as England, following on, lost Gooch without a run on the board before bad light caused a long delay – much to the annoyance of the large crowd. Annoyance turned to anger when the umpires, wearing their blazers, came out at five minutes to six, called for the covers and abandoned play for the day. Almost immediately the light improved and with Headingley suddenly bathed in sunshine, the crowd made their feelings known in no uncertain terms.

One had a great deal of sympathy for them. A Saturday crowd at Leeds invariably includes a fair representation from Scotland, Durham and Northumberland where chances to watch first-class cricket, let alone Test cricket, are extremely limited and they believed, quite rightly, that they had been short-changed.

Ladbrokes, the bookmakers, who are seldom likely to be short-changed, were now offering odds of 500 to 1 against an English victory, and a couple of members of the Australian team, soon to be revealed as Dennis Lillee and Rodney Marsh, were quick to snap them up. I am certain that they had no ulterior motive. There are always people who cannot resist such odds and if they can afford to lose 50p or £1 then so be it. An Australian who likes a flutter is unlikely to be restricted to such a small stake, however, so this turned out to be quite a betting coup.

By mid-afternoon on Monday, there must have been justification for the odds to be extended to 1,000 to 1 – not that Ladbrokes were about to do it! – as England collapsed again to 135 for seven, still 92 behind with only Old, who had got a duck in the first innings, and Willis to come. Players, officials and the media in general had booked out of their hotels. Nothing, it seemed, could prevent Australia winning with a day to spare.

Only Geoff Boycott had offered any serious resistance, defending skilfully for three and a half hours against the sustained accuracy of Lillee and Alderman and looking most aggrieved when an lbw decision brought his innings to a close for 46. It looked all over, but then came one of the most incredible innings ever played. In the next three hours, Ian Botham so utterly destroyed the hitherto all-conquering Australian attack that Lillee, Alderman and Lawson were reduced to complete disarray.

Botham's immense strength and perfect timing were irresistible as he plundered the pacemen and scattered the fielders to distant parts of the famous arena. And he was not alone in this sudden bombardment. His partner, the left-handed Graham Dilley, for the most part standing bolt upright and thrusting his right leg down the pitch, gave his adversaries the sight of a full flow of the bat and mercifully played and hit straight. Their partnership yielded 117 astonishing runs in just 80 minutes for the eighth wicket before Dilley departed, bowled by Alderman for a valiant 56.

Then it was Chris Old's turn to support the rampaging Botham as he cracked on towards the most memorable of his Test centuries. Another left-hander, the Yorkshireman had never made full use of his natural talent with the bat, but this time, inspired by what had gone before, he helped Botham to add another 67 priceless runs. And even when he was out, bowled by Lawson, Willis survived the final 20 minutes so that a remarkable day ended with Botham undefeated on 149 and England, who should have been dead and buried long before, finding themselves 124 runs to the good.

Once again the hotel switchboards were busy as everyone checked back in again, though on the face of it Australia remained very hot favourites. With their bowlers refreshed by a night's rest and only one wicket to take, a deficit of 124 did not seem to present any great difficulty, particularly bearing in mind that England's last three wickets had already produced 216 runs.

Botham added just four to his overnight score on the final day before Willis was taken in the slips by Allan Border, leaving Australia to score only 130 to go two-up in the series. And it looked like a comparatively easy task as Wood took advantage of two wayward overs from Dilley, who shared the new ball with Botham, to move quickly into double figures.

With the score on 13, Wood was caught behind by Bob Taylor off Botham, but when Willis rather surprisingly replaced Dilley at the Football Stand End where he had to bowl against a stiffish breeze, the tall Warwickshire fast bowler did not look at his best – or indeed his happiest. Obviously concerned with his first innings analysis of nought for 72, not to mention a spate of no balls, he was taken on one side by Brearley who obviously understood his predicament.

'Have a crack at the Kirkstall End,' he said, or words to this effect. 'It's slightly downhill, with the wind. And forget about the no balls. I'm not concerned with them. Just let it go and give me all you've got.'

It was brilliant psychology and brilliant captaincy, and it simply inspired big Bob. With his own mind put at rest, he did exactly what he had been asked to do, with startling results. In the next hour we witnessed a spell of hostile fast bowling on a par with anything achieved by the dynamic Australian duo of Lillee and Thomson or the famed West Indian quartet of Holding, Roberts, Garner and Croft.

Willis bowled like a man possessed, as though his very life depended on it, and for once he was supported by some quite magnificent English catching and fielding.

From 56 for one, Australia crashed to 75 for eight – and Willis took six of those wickets in no time at all.

Australia still needed only 55 to win and there were some agonizing moments as Lillee and Ray Bright made 35 of them in only four overs with some desperate swings. But Willis had the last word, getting Lillee to spoon the ball towards mid-on where Mike Gatting raced in and dived to hold a superb catch and then hitting Bright's middle stump with a yorker.

So England clinched one of the most astonishing victories of all time by a margin of 18 runs. It was the first time this century – and only the second time in Test history – that a side had won after being forced to follow on. It was a triumph for Mike Brearley, recalled to captain England and doing the job in masterly fashion. It was a triumph for Bob Willis, whose final figures of eight for 43 were the best of his career and a just reward for a superb piece of fast bowling. But above all it was a triumph for Ian Botham.

On his return to the ranks, he had proved he remained the most inspirational cricketer of his day by scoring 199 runs for once out, taking seven wickets and overcoming what appeared to be insurmountable odds. It was just the tonic everyone needed.

Two days later, I pronounced myself fit to return to the commentary box and I was at Edgbaston to see Botham produce another extraordinary performance – with the ball this time – to give England another narrow victory in the fourth Test. Australia, needing only 151 to win, were coasting home at 105 for four when Botham polished them off for 121 with an incredible spell of five wickets for one run.

And even then he was not finished with poor Kim Hughes and his, by now, shell-shocked troops. In the fifth Test at Old Trafford, where England retained the Ashes, he took his third successive man-of-the-match award after scoring what must surely rank as the most spectacular century even seen in Test cricket. His 118 runs came in 123 minutes, the last 90 of them in a mere 53 minutes.

And he hammered six sixes – a record in Test matches between England and Australia – and 13 fours.

So what manner of man is he? And how good a cricketer? Well, at times, I can see a touch of the Wally Hammond, the Keith Miller and the Ted Dexter about him – and that cannot be bad for a start. Yet he is very much a man of the eighties in thoughts, words and deeds. He has obviously played his cricket at the right time. Before the war and in the early years afterwards, the professional game was hamstrung with conventions and beggarly financial rewards and he would have had problems leading his particular way of life.

But I totally disagree with many of my contemporaries who are still suspicious of his great talent and believe that much of the opposition he has faced has been second rate. The so-called golden years had their full quota of second-raters and I am firmly convinced that Botham's star would have shone just as brightly no matter when and against whom he played his cricket.

He has already given us all countless hours of pleasure. Long may he continue to do so.

THREE GREAT GAMES
AUSTRALIA

J. Dyson b Dilley	102	c Taylor b Willis	34
G. M. Wood lbw b Botham	34	c Taylor b Botham	10
T. M. Chappell c Taylor b Willey	27	c Taylor b Willis	8
K. J. Hughes c and b Botham	89	c Botham b Willis	0
R. J. Bright b Dilley	7	b Willis	19
G. N. Yallop c Taylor b Botham	58	c Gatting b Willis	0
A. R. Border lbw b Botham	8	b Old	0
R. W. Marsh b Botham	28	c Dilley b Willis	4
G. F. Lawson c Taylor b Botham	13	c Taylor b Willis	1
D. K. Lillee not out	3	c Gatting b Willis	17
T. M. Alderman not out	0	not out	0
B 4, LB 13, W 3, NB 12	32	LB3, W1, NB 14	18
(9 wkts dec.)	401		111

England Bowling

	O	M	R	W	O	M	R	W
Willis	30	8	72	0	15.1	3	43	8
Old	43	14	91	0	9	1	21	1
Dilley	27	4	78	2	2	0	11	0
Botham	39.2	11	95	6	7	3	14	1
Willey	13	2	31	1	3	1	4	0
Boycott	3	2	2	0				

Fall of wickets

1/55 2/149 3/196 4/220 5/332   1/13 2/56 3/58 4/58 5/65
6/354 7/357 8/396 9/401   6/68 7/74 8/75 9/110 10/111

ENGLAND

G. A. Gooch lbw b Alderman	2	c Alderman b Lillee	0
G. Boycott b Lawson	12	lbw b Alderman	46
J. M. Brearley c Marsh b Alderman	10	c Alderman b Lillee	14
D. I. Gower c Marsh b Lawson	24	c Border b Alderman	9
M. W. Gatting lbw b Lillee	15	lbw b Alderman	1
P. Willey b Lawson	8	c Dyson b Lillee	33
I. T. Botham c Marsh b Lillee	50	not out	149
R. W. Taylor c Marsh b Lillee	5	c Bright b Alderman	1
G. R. Dilley c b Lillee	13	b Alderman	56
C. M. Old c Border b Alderman	0	b Lawson	29
R. G. D. Willis not out	1	c Border b Alderman	2
B 6, LB 11, W 6, NB 11	34	B 5, LB 3, W 3, NB 5	16
	174		356

Australian Bowling

	O	M	R	W	O	M	R	W
Lillee	18.5	7	49	4	25	6	94	3
Alderman	19	4	59	3	35.3	6	135	6
Lawson	13	3	32	3	23	4	96	1
Bright					4	0	15	0

Fall of wickets

1/12 2/40 3/42 4/84 5/87   1/0 2/18 3/37 4/41 5/105
6/112 7/148 8/166 9/167 10/174   6/133 7/135 8/252 9/319 10/356

Umpires: B. J. Meyer and D. G. L. Evans.

6

In Comparison

For all the changes that have taken place in the game of cricket, I have always maintained that good players would have been good players in whatever era they appeared. Good batsmen would always have scored runs; good bowlers would always have taken wickets.

People of my generation, including many of my illustrious England contemporaries, will probably consider it sacrilege for me to talk in the same breath of Sir Leonard Hutton and Geoffrey Boycott, Freddie Trueman and Bob Willis, Keith Miller and Ian Botham, Peter May and David Gower, Tony Lock and Derek Underwood, Godfrey Evans and Bob Taylor, Richie Benaud and Mike Brearley. But times have changed and I would never attempt to disparage the performances of the present-day players who have rather more complex problems to face than we ever did.

Laker and Emburey

To illustrate the point, let me start this series of comparisons by admitting that I would have found it much more difficult to break into first-class cricket in the eighties than I did in the fifties. When I joined the Surrey staff, the county's season consisted of 33 three-day matches played on uncovered wickets. There was no such thing as one-day cricket. And every encouragement was given to the young spin bowler.

A look at the first-class averages for 1954 shows how many of them took advantage of the situation. Bob Appleyard, an off-spin bowler of uncommon pace, and Johnny

Wardle both took more than 150 wickets; I had 135 and Tony Lock 125. And also figuring high on the list were the likes of Jim McConnon, Roy Tattersall, Fred Titmus, Alan Oakman, Jack Young, John Mortimore, Bomber Wells, Johnny Lawrence, Edwin Smith, Doug Wright, Eric Hollies, Sam Cook and Malcolm Hilton.

You can only gain confidence as a spin bowler by taking wickets, and in those days you got far more chances to bowl in helpful conditions than you do now. You might struggle for a couple of weeks on good wickets but generally in an English summer you were soon going to come across a rain-affected wicket when it was not uncommon for a good spin bowler to pick up seven or eight wickets. The same would apply if you were fortunate enough to bowl on one of the lesser-known grounds where the wickets were not so good. On top of that, it was rare in county sides to find anyone after no. 8 having any great pretensions as a batsman; in fact they were little more than rabbits. Gloucester, for example, could guarantee half a dozen cheap wickets in a match by courtesy of F. D. McHugh, Cook and Wells. These days, nos. 9, 10 and jack tend to come in and push up and down with a straight bat.

At the outset of my career, I used to bowl the same way on every type of wicket because I believed the only way to succeed as a spin bowler was to spin the ball as much as I could. I had the advantage of being able to spin it more than anyone else at the time and would concentrate on bowling accurately with the spin. It meant that on good wickets I was reasonably economical and if the pitch was at all helpful I was able to come into my own.

One of the reasons why there has been such a dearth of top-class off-spinners in recent years is their unwillingness to stick to a basic method with the right degree of patience. Pat Pocock, who is as talented as any England have produced in the past 20 years and must have considered himself unlucky to have played in no more than 17 Test matches, all but three of them abroad, until his recall in 1984, is a prime example. Even at the start of his career, he was prone to too much variation which, for an inexperienced bowler, usually meant at least one bad ball an over. The same criticism applies to New Zealand's John Bracewell, who obviously has a lot of ability but on the last England tour was guilty of trying to do too much too soon.

Significantly, the most successful off-spinners in recent years have been people like Titmus, Illingworth and Lance Gibbs, who all learned their trade in the fifties, though I have been very impressed with the development of John Emburey, whom I now consider to be the best in the world.

It was far from easy for Emburey to break into county cricket in the early seventies. He had played for Surrey Young Cricketers in 1969 and 1970 but was then allowed to join Middlesex where he had to wait until 1973 to make his debut. It was not until Titmus retired – and ironically joined Surrey as coach – that he was able to establish himself in 1977, by which time he was 25. He would certainly have got his opportunity a lot earlier in the fifties.

As an off-spin bowler, Emburey is somewhere in between Hugh Tayfield, who took 170 Test wickets for South Africa, and myself in that he spins it rather more than Tayfield did but not as much as I did. His height is an advantage because it enables him to get extra bounce and he is also blessed with a good temperament which means he can take the kind of hammer that so easily undermines the inferior bowler. His successes in Australia and South Africa show that he has the technique to adjust to different wickets which I always found to be the most difficult part of the off-spinner's art.

It goes without saying that Emburey has been badly missed by England after being suspended for three years for taking part in the rebel tour of South Africa. But, happily, his best years should still be ahead of him. In fact he should now be approaching his peak if my experience is anything to go by. I believe that I was in my thirties before I reached my best, and that I bowled as well as I ever did in my life on the 1958–9 tour of Australia when I was nearly 37.

Now, 25 years on, I am forever being asked how I think I would have coped with the demands made on the modern off-spinner; how I think I would have adapted to bowling in a five-day Test and a 40-over knockabout on a Sunday afternoon. I would like to be able to say that it would not have made a scrap of difference to the way I bowled. But clearly that would be nonsense. I have given it a lot of thought, and come to the conclusion that I would have had to cope in the same way as people like Emburey and Pocock have done by increasing their pace and bowling a fuller length at middle stump or middle and leg. In all honesty I cannot think of any other answer to the off-spinner's problem. If I bowled as I used to do in a county match with three men out on the fence, I would back myself to take five wickets. But those five wickets would probably cost me 60 runs. Limited-overs cricket is more about containment than bowling sides out, and one for 25 would be a far better performance.

Lock and Underwood

Unlike John Emburey and myself, who had to wait until we were 25 before establishing ourselves in first-class cricket, Tony Lock and Derek Underwood had both taken more than 1,000 wickets by the time they were that age. But that – and the fact that they both practised their own, very individual brands of left-arm spin – is all they did have in common.

Lock, the firebrand, bowled with an aggression not normally associated with slow bowlers, intimidating the batsmen with shouts and gestures. And he was just as belligerent when he was not bowling, taking some incredible catches, most frequently at backward short leg but most memorably off his own bowling. Underwood, though just as ruthless professionally, seemed almost mechanical by comparison. Always cool, calm and collected, he seemed as much of a gentleman on the field as he is off it and rarely showed any emotion. And he had to put in a lot of hard work to make himself a reliable outfielder.

It was in 1946, at the age of 17, that Lock began what for me was the most remarkable of all cricket careers. What made it so was the fact that he managed to change his action completely three times and remain at the top of his profession.

He started as a slow, flighty bowler who could not spin the ball at all. He used to bowl with a deep extra cover and a long off and get his wickets by having people stumped or caught in the deep. Whenever we came across a wicket that was turning, I would take six or seven wickets and he would be lucky to pick up one or two, usually caught in the covers having a dash at him.

Yet Locky was always a very ambitious guy and at the end of one season he came up to me and asked if I could help him to spin the ball. I said I would be delighted as long as he got permission from the coach, Andrew Sandham, because in those days you had to have permission before you could do anything. Andrew agreed, albeit a little grudgingly, and I spent the best part of two weeks in the nets, showing Lock how to spin the ball, explaining that he had to get his fingers round it and give it a flick and warning that if he was really going to spin it, it would hurt because he would get sore fingers.

Locky, tough, competitive character that he was, went off to Allders cricket school at Croydon where he was working that winter and began to put into practice what we had been talking about. The only problem was that the net was not high enough so that when he got his arm up and let the ball go it would hit the top of the net, and the only way he could counter this was to bowl with a bent arm! Now you can bowl with a bent arm as long as it remains bent all the way through, but Lock got himself into such a state when he saw he was making the ball turn for the first time in his life that his arm did not stay bent. It developed into a straight arm and into a jerk.

He continued bowling like that all through the winter and I will never forget the day we reported back to the Oval for pre-season nets. Jack Parker called me over to watch Lock bowling. We stood behind the net where he was propelling the ball at something approaching medium

86

pace and not only turning it about a foot but making it
lift as well on what was not a particularly bad wicket. It
was quite remarkable.

'What do you think?' asked Jack.

'It looks suspicious to me,' I replied.

'I'm bloody sure it's suspicious,' said Parker.

'Well, what do we do about it?' I asked him.

'It's not for us to say anything,' said Jack. 'And anyway
it could save us a lot of time in the field, you know.'

That was the start of Lock's second action, and he got
away with it for something like five years during which
time he picked up around 1,000 first-class wickets. On a
pitch that was slightly helpful, he got a lot of people out.
On a pitch that was very helpful, he was unplayable. Yet
when the pitch was not helpful at all, he was still a pretty
ordinary bowler, as he discovered in Australia in 1958–9
when he played in four Tests on hard, flat wickets and
took just five wickets for 375.

It was in New Zealand at the end of that tour that he
saw for the first time film of himself bowling – and he
was quite horrified. He had had a few previous skirmishes,
of course. Umpire Fred Price had called him for throwing
in England. And he was no-balled three times on one day
against Barbados on the 1953–4 tour of West Indies. In
fact one of those occasions produced the funniest incident
I have ever seen on a cricket ground. It was the first time
we had come across Gary Sobers, then aged 18, and it
was not long before Locky let him have his 'quickie' which
flattened his middle stump. Sobers, who had not been
halfway through his backlift when the ball fizzed past,
put his head down and was almost level with Lock on his
sad walk back to the pavilion when there was a shout of
'no ball' from the square-leg umpire. So Gary put his
gloves back on and returned to the crease to resume his
innings.

But it was that film clip in New Zealand which eventually persuaded Lock that he had to change his action once
more, and it was a case of third time lucky. Within the
space of six months he had got it back to something
like his original style but at the same time had actually

managed to increase his power of spin. And from then on, right until the end of his career, I believe he was not only a legitimate bowler but also a quite magnificent one.

It was almost a fairy story when he emigrated to Australia, took over as captain and coach of Western Australia, and led them to their first honours in first-class cricket. His captaincy was quite exceptional and he broke all the Australian wicket-taking records. England really did not see the best of him, though he did return to lead Leicestershire and put them on the road to recovery by convincing them that they could actually play the game. In the end, he was a hell of a cricketer.

Underwood has been almost as remarkable a bowler, though for vastly different reasons. He, too, was only 17 when he started but he came straight out of club cricket with Beckenham to take more than 100 wickets in his first season for Kent. He was the youngest player ever to do that and many people thought he would struggle to do it again as batsmen grew more accustomed to his unorthodox style.

They were wrong. He has gone on taking wickets, picking up more than 100 in a season for the tenth time in 1983. And if he had not exiled himself from Test cricket, first by signing a three-year contract with Kerry Packer's World Series Cricket in Australia, then by incurring a three-year ban by playing with the 'rebels' in South Africa, he would be the top wicket-taker in Test history.

It has always been difficult to categorize his bowling which is in complete contrast to Lock's – in any of the latter's three styles. You cannot call Underwood a left-arm spinner; nor can you call him a medium-pacer. The only thing to do, I suppose, is to call him a very high-class bowler.

I must have watched him bowl hundreds and hundreds of overs and the number of times he has bowled badly could be counted on the fingers of one hand. His accuracy in terms of length and direction is as consistent as anything I have ever seen, just about flawless. On good wickets, the good batsmen can play him all day long for the simple reason that he is not a particularly big spinner of the ball. In fact his method is more of a roll and a cut. But they will always have the greatest difficult scoring runs off him because of his uncanny accuracy. And as soon as he gets on a wicket that gives him the slightest degree of help, he can be unplayable. The usual answer when the ball is turning is for the batsman to try to get on the attack, but Underwood is too quick through the air to make that possible and any attempt to hit him against the spin usually means sudden death.

In contrast to most of the top spin bowlers – and they certainly include Lock – Underwood is at his most dangerous on wet wickets rather than dusty ones. Just how deadly he can be was perfectly illustrated in the final Test against Australia at the Oval in 1968. A storm flooded the ground at lunchtime on the last day and by the time groundsman Ted Warn, helped by volunteers from the crowd, had mopped up, only 75 minutes remained for England to take Australia's last five wickets. They struggled for 40 minutes to get even one because the pitch was so dead, but once Basil d'Oliveira had broken through Underwood found the drying surface ideal for his purpose and captured the last four wickets for six runs in 27 balls. England won by 226 runs with six minutes to spare to save the series, though Australia kept the Ashes.

There have been isolated occasions at the Oval during fine hot spells when the wicket has dusted in the last two days and there has been the opportunity for the spinner to take advantage but Underwood has been unable to do it. He was well aware of this weakness, of course, and for a while he tried to change his style by bowling much slower and giving the ball more air. But he was far from happy doing it and I am sure he was wise to revert to the style he knew best.

For the purists, that has always been a bit too quick. Yet in the days before the law caught up with him, Lock would bowl just as fast as Underwood has ever done and still make the ball spin like a top. So much so that at Surrey we used to say that when Alec Bedser came off and Locky came on, gully had to go back a yard!

Trueman and Willis

It is said that when Fred Trueman became the first England bowler to take 300 Test wickets, he was of the opinion that whoever broke his record would be "bloody tired". Well, Bob Willis did not seem at all tired when he passed Fred's haul of 307 against New Zealand in the first Test of the 1984 tour, and Dennis Lillee's world record of 355 seemed well within his reach until he was sadly struck down by a mysterious virus infection in Pakistan, which precipitated his retirement from first-class cricket at the end of the following season.

Trueman and Willis have nothing in common. Frederick Sewards Trueman, 5ft. 10in. tall and stockily built, was simply born to be a fast bowler. Robert George Dylan Willis, 6ft. 6in. high and as thin as a lath, had to will himself to do the job – with the help of a hypnotist.

Fred never had any doubts in his mind. There was no way he was ever going to be a left-arm spinner. As the son of a steeplechase jockey who got too heavy and finished up working down a coal mine, he had been endowed with all the requisites of a fast bowler. Over the years, a height of between 5ft. 9in. and 6ft. had proved just about right for the great speed merchants – men like Larwood, Lindwall, Tyson and Statham. On top of that, Fred was immensely strong in the legs and shoulders. His mental attitude was just right for his chosen profession. And his action was quite superb.

The first time I saw him, I think, was in the 1950 Test trial at Bradford when he was only 19 and still uncapped by Yorkshire. My recollection is a bit vague because I have personal reasons for remembering that match, but I do seem to remember him coming on third change – Les Jackson and Eric Bedser opened the bowling – and making an immediate impact by bowling Len Hutton!

Fred was a bit raw in those days. He hardly seemed to know his own strength so that when he was fielding on the boundary there would often be five Yorkshiremen in a line backing up because they had no idea how far he was going to throw the ball! But the basics were already there, and to my mind they never changed from the first time I played with him until the last at Melbourne in 1959.

His classical, sideways-on action gave him the ability to bowl the out-swinger which was far and away his best delivery throughout his career. It was only in later years when he reduced his pace considerably that he was able to cut the ball back. And despite what Fred might say – and he once reckoned that he probably moved the ball more than any other pace bowler in the history of the game – he bowled a fair percentage which did not deviate at all, in common with all bowlers, great and not so great.

One of my most vivid recollections of Fred goes back to the Trent Bridge Test against the West Indies in 1957 when the selectors misguidedly left out Tony Lock, giving us only four specialist bowlers on a beautiful batting wicket in very hot weather. It hardly seemed to matter when Tom Graveney made his highest score of 258 in an England total of 619 for six declared. But after we had forced the West Indies to follow on Trevor Bailey ricked his back, so that Brian Statham finished up bowling 70 overs in the match, Fred 65 and me 105. Collie Smith, tragically killed only two years later in a car crash which his great friend Gary Sobers was lucky to survive, saved the match with 169. The only time he looked in any trouble was just after Fred took the second – or was it the third? – new ball. He was getting a bit of stick from the spectators at the Radcliffe Road end and one of them bellowed out: 'Trueman, you're not as quick as bloody Laker!' Duly inspired, Fred promptly unleashed three superb out-swingers on the trot, each of which had Smith playing and missing. After the third, Fred stood in the middle of the pitch, arms akimbo, hair in his eyes, glowering at the batsman. 'Smith,' he roared, 'you're playing in Ireland tomorrow but there'll be no need for you to catch the plane. You could bloody walk over there and beat 'em.'

Fred was not the quickest bowler I ever saw. Without question, that was Frank Tyson who for a period of two years bowled as fast as anyone can ever have done. He was an intelligent guy who had decided that he was going

91

to go flat out for two years rather than carry on for 20 years and finish up as a medium pacer. He achieved his speed through sheer physical strength – derived from an enormous pair of shoulders, strong legs and a powerful back – a long delivery stride and an arm like a catapult which came over in a huge arc before letting the ball go at top velocity. He burned himself out, of course, but not before he had won the Ashes for Len Hutton with 28 wickets in the 1954–5 series.

Tyson, like Trueman, was lucky to have Brian Statham bowling at the other end. The old greyhound, as we called him, just bowled fast and straight, working on the theory that if the batsman missed, he hit. And in my opinion he was probably as good as either of them.

Willis never had the benefit of that kind of support during his finest years. And he has also been at a disadvantage in spending most of his career bowling on covered wickets. He has not come across many like the rain-affected pitch on which Trueman destroyed India with eight for 31 at Old Trafford in 1952.

In such circumstances, the commitment he has shown in spearheading England's attack virtually single-handed, the courage with which he has overcome a sickening succession of injuries, and the character that finally made him England's captain are qualities which have earned him a place right up alongside the great fast bowlers of the past. Indeed I doubt if any of them could have emulated him.

Willis has never looked the part. He has always had to work hard at his game and it took him a long time to become a consistently good Test match bowler. For years, his long, ungainly run-up which came round in a half-circle and his ugly, open-chested action made it impossible for him to do any more than swing the ball in to the right-handed batsman. And I well remember Hampshire's West Indian Roy Marshall giving him a painful lesson one day at Southampton by walking across outside off stump almost every ball and putting him away down on the long-leg boundary.

It was only when Willis straightened out his run that

his bowling improved by about 50 per cent. His action was still not the prettiest but with his height and high arm action he was often able to get that extra bit of bounce which is so vital. And it is probable that his overall record – especially in county cricket – would have been even better if Surrey had given him his county cap before he was flown out to Australia to replace the injured Alan Ward in 1970.

Stuart Surridge was then chairman of the county's cricket committee and his reluctance to come to terms with the ambitious young fast bowler led to a prolonged dispute which ended with Willis eventually joining Warwickshire. With a bit more foresight, he would have played his cricket at the Oval, and no doubt enjoyed more success than he has done pounding away on the unhelpful Edgbaston wicket.

In some recent summers, he has bowled more overs and taken more wickets for England than he has for Warwickshire, and his detractors, particularly those in the Birmingham area, are quick to suggest that he has rarely shown the same commitment to his county as he has to his country. But even they must marvel at the tenacity of a man who seemed finished in 1975, when major surgery on both knees was further complicated by a blood clot which threatened rather more than his career, and again in 1981 when he was flown home from the West Indies for yet another knee operation.

What he has achieved since then is quite remarkable. I cannot say that he has altered my view that it is not a good idea to have a fast bowler as captain. But as a bowler he has surpassed even the great Fred Trueman in one respect. As Fred got older, he got slower and had to rely more on guile than pace. The extraordinary thing about Bob Willis was that in his thirty-fifth year he was still capable of bowling as fast as he had ever done.

Hutton and Boycott

At the risk of provoking another outbreak of civil unrest in Yorkshire, I have to confess that I have idolized Sir Leonard Hutton ever since I was a schoolboy, and if

Geoffrey Boycott carries on playing until he is 90, he will never surpass him in my estimation. When I was 14, I could sit and watch Hutton bat all day. And though he was only 19 himself, he was quite capable of doing it.

His batting technique was the best I have ever seen. He had every shot in the book, although on occasions he was loathe to use all of them. The key was his footwork which I believe to be the most essential part of batting. Whether he was attacking or defending, Len's was a joy to watch. Once you get your feet in the right position – and in Hutton's case the initial movement was usually slightly back and across with the right foot – what follows seems to be that much easier.

I think his greatest joy was in his cover and off driving which were masterpieces of placement and timing. I can still vividly recall a century he made against Surrey at the Oval when he almost reduced Tony Lock to tears. He would move to the pitch of a ball slightly outside off stump and hit it gloriously through extra cover. To counter that, Tony would move his extra cover a bit straighter, so Hutton would delay his shot just a fraction of a second and hit it four or five yards squarer. In fact Hutton was able to play this shot anywhere in an arc stretching from point to mid-off.

Most top batsmen over the years have agreed that the most difficult deliveries to play are the late out-swinger and the variations of the top-class leg-spinner – and nobody has played them better than Len Hutton. This was because he was able to delay his stroke until the last possible moment to take into account the swing or the spin, whereas less-gifted players tend to commit themselves too early. If there was a chink in Hutton's armour, it was surprisingly against the in-swing or off-break bowler. And I have often wondered whether this could have had something to do with his wartime accident as a PT instructor which left him with his left arm weaker and fractionally shorter than his right.

It certainly affected his hooking. In his early days he used to play the shot magnificently. But later on he just about eliminated it, even when he was on the receiving end of as many bouncers as any batsman of his day. Lindwall and Miller, especially, gave him a torrid time when they were at their fastest and it is a further tribute to his remarkable footwork that I cannot ever recall him being hit.

Having said that, however, I do not believe he ever had to face the kind of sustained, short-pitched hostility which confronted Boycott on his return to Test cricket in 1977 after his self-imposed three-year exile. When most of the top fast bowlers were playing in Kerry Packer's World Series Cricket, former England captain Tony Greig made the jibe that Boycott had deliberately avoided them. But that lie was nailed in 1980 and 1981 when Boycott took on the Australians and the West Indians in successive series at home and abroad without ever backing away. In fact I have never detected any shortage of courage in Boycott's make-up and would suggest that his technique against such fearsome batteries of fast bowling as Holding, Roberts, Croft and Garner of the West Indies and Lillee, Thomson, Lawson and Hogg of Australia was vastly superior to that shown by anyone else.

Yet highly as I regard Boycott's batting, I do not think he has ever achieved the stature of Hutton for two reasons. First, he has never had to face up to the class of spin bowling that confronted Hutton; second, he has never had as many shots as Hutton, who was consequently a much more fluent scorer.

The tragedy of this is that Boycott could have been a far more prolific stroke-player, for there have been few greater one-day innings than his 146, including three sixes and 15 fours, against Surrey at a waterlogged Lord's in the 1965 Gillette Cup Final.

Whereas Hutton was a natural batsman, a schoolboy prodigy who made his first-class debut at 17, Boycott is a self-made cricketer who did not get into the Yorkshire first team until he was 22, a year older than Hutton was when he made his 364 against Australia. But there are certain similarities. Like Boycott, Hutton went out to open the batting with every intention of staying all day. But whereas Boycott will be upset all day if he gets out early, Len's disappointment would not last much longer than half an hour. Like Boycott, Hutton was also a bit of an introvert. But, again, he did not take it quite to the same extreme as Geoffrey.

No one, not even Boycott, has ever taken his cricket more seriously than Hutton did. Naturally he was very raw at the start of his career and it took him some time to adjust to a completely different way of life from the one he had known as a carpenter's son at Pudsey. But he educated himself through cricket. A careful man in every way, he gave a great deal of thought to everything he did. Even when he was England's captain, he would lie awake at night, wondering and probably worrying about what he was going to do next day.

He had some extraordinary theories about the game, one of them being that you needed brown eyes to make runs in the West Indies. All the great batsmen of the Caribbean from Weekes, Worrell and Walcott to Sobers, Lloyd and Richards have tended to prove his point, I suppose. But I don't know what he made of it when the blue-eyed David Gower played one of his finest innings – 154 not out – in Kingston, Jamaica, in 1981!

Nor has Len ever been the kind of man to give too much away, as my Surrey colleague Micky Stewart discovered during his early days at the Oval. Micky, who had not been in the game very long, was worried about some particular aspect of his batting so when I saw Hutton approaching I thought it would be a good opportunity for the youngster to learn something. Having made the introductions I left them to it and was pleased to see them deep in conversation for a good half-hour.

When Micky came back, I said: 'Well, let's hear it, then. What have you learned?'

Stewart looked puzzled. 'He just talked on and on about the new lbw rule,' he said, shaking his head. 'I'm no wiser about my batting now than I was before.'

Hutton kept his opinions to himself when he became England's first professional captain, sensibly taking no part in the fierce controversy that raged over such a break

...art Surridge (*above*), quite simply the best ...ptain I ever played with, and Richie ...naud (*right*) (tossing with Frank Worrell ...ring Australia's memorable 1960-61 series ...ainst the West Indies), who is very ...mfortably the best I ever played against ... ...indeed have ever seen

...low: The gospel according to Fred Trueman, seen preaching in the nets before a Test ...atch at Lord's to Gubby Allen, Peter May and Frank Tyson

Above: E. W. 'Jim' Swanton, who left an indelible mark on cricket reporting and probably exerted more influence on the game from the Press Box than anyone else has done

Left: John Arlott, the best of all broadcasters. It was a sad day when he retired from the commentary box. Can he ever be replaced?

Brian Johnston, the youngest septuagenarian I have ever met. No one has ever waxed more enthusiastically about the game that has been his life

Neville Cardus, the most readable of all the game's authors. One may have doubted his technical knowledge but you could not help but be swayed by his affection for cricket – and especially Lancashire cricket

ou could pick a fair old side from this galaxy of cricketers at Gubby Allen's eightieth birthday
arty. *Left to right (back):* M. J. K. Smith, E. R. Dexter, T. W. Graveney, A. V. Bedser,
. R. Brown, B. L. d'Oliveira; (*front*): F. G. Mann, T. G. Evans, D. C. S. Compton, Sir L. Hutton,
. O. Allen, L. E. G. Ames, P. B. H. May, J. C. Laker

n the board. The first editorial conference of *Wisden Cricket Monthly. Left to right:* Patrick
agar, Ted Dexter, Jim Laker, editor David Frith, John Arlott, Bob Willis and David Gower

Above: Hollywood 1957 ... Greeting my old friend Boris Karloff –a lifelong cricket fan and a much nicer man than he appeared in all those horror movies – when he was featured in 'This is Your Life'

Below: Saying thanks ... to show-business personalities Frank Muir, Dorothy Tutin, Rober Powell and Michael Meyer for their efforts in raising money for the Ken Barrington Memori Appeal

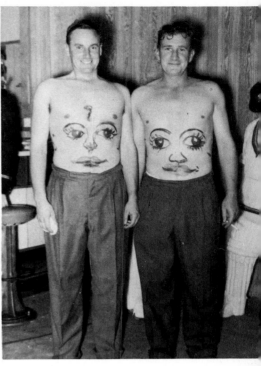

ess who? Tweedledum and Tweedledee
ning a prize in the fancy-dress
npetition on the ship taking the England
m to South Africa in 1956.
is revealed ... England's captain
3. H. May and his off-spinner!

low: Together again ... John Arlott and I admire a collection of porcelain figures of
nous cricketers

Above: At the races – presenting a prize to a lucky owner at Lingfield Park in 1981. I cannot remember the horse's name … only that I didn't back it!

Below: Lord's Taverner's Day at Newmarket … and another loser coming up from tipster Willie Rushton

l Frindall, England's No 1 cricket
tistician, who has brought a new
mension to the business of scoring ... and
rned a good living from it, too

Happy memories at Old Trafford – with my
old friend Bert Flack, the groundsman who
Australia believed produced the perfect
pitch for me in 1956

ck at work with B B C T V producer Bill Taylor and fellow commentator Ted Dexter

Press gang. English and Australian cricket writers take a break in Tasmania during the 1982-83 tour. *Left to right:* Jim Gill (England supporter), Graham Otway (*Press Association*), Steve Whiting (*Sun*), Matthew Engel (*Guardian*), Tom Prior (Melbourne *Sun*), Mrs Marlar, Dick Tucker (Sydney *Daily Mirror*), Peter Laker (London *Daily Mirror*), Peter Smith (*Daily Mail*), Karl Kershaw (*Sunday People* – partially hidden), Michael Carey (*Daily Telegraph*), Phil Wilkins (*The Australian*), Peter Baxter (BBC producer), Mrs Baxter, John Thicknesse (London *Standard*), Brian Bearshaw (Manchester *Evening News*), Pat Gibson (*Daily Express*), Robin Marlar (*Sunday Times*)

Press relations. England cricketers John Emburey and Graham Gooch and *Daily Express* correspondent Pat Gibson sample Indian hospitality at Baroda on the 1981-82 tour. Richard Streeton of *The Times* is on the left

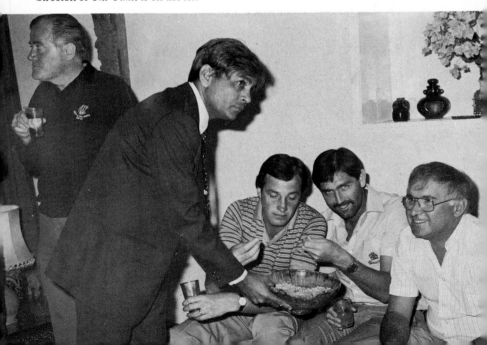

with tradition. But he was a proud man. And, as one might have expected, he did a typically professional job.

I do not think he rated me very highly at the time and consequently I had a few ups and downs with him. But later on in his reign, he went to the other extreme and I felt that I could do no wrong. It took me a long time to convince him that I could bowl, mainly because he was not too interested in spin bowling. He had been through the fast bowling fire of Lindwall, Miller and big Bill Johnston so that when he got the opportunity to lead England with Trueman, Statham and Tyson at his command, he relished the possibilities. And it was one of the greatest moments of his life when he returned home with the Ashes after Tyson and Statham had destroyed Australia in 1954–5.

But the great thing about Hutton as a captain was that whatever he thought about them professionally the players liked him – and I'm afraid that could not be said about Boycott for most of his time in charge at Yorkshire and in the three Tests in which he led England after Mike Brearley had broken his arm. Boycott simply could not abide failure – or even the thought of failure – and sadly that paranoia has always seemed to affect the people around him.

May and Gower

It was somewhat appropriate that Peter May should have been chairman of the England selectors when David Gower was appointed captain in 1984. For there are certain similarities between the two, even though the former was a tall, cultured right-hander from Charterhouse, Cambridge University and Surrey and the latter is an elegant, blond-haired left-hander from King's School, Canterbury, London University and Leicestershire.

Both of them were well educated at good cricketing schools before going on to university; both of them succeeded to the captaincy of their country when they were still in their mid-twenties; and both of them were hailed as the finest batsmen of their generation.

But while Gower may be the best batsman England

have produced in recent years, there is no doubt in my mind that May is the best batsman we have had since the 1939-45 war.

Peter Barker Howard May had more competition, for a start. Among his contemporaries were the likes of Ted Dexter, Colin Cowdrey, Tom Graveney and Ken Barrington, yet from the day he picked up a cricket bat for the first time it was obvious that he was something special.

I think that nearly all great batsmen are born not made – very few, though there have been one or two, become great as a result of intensive coaching – and Peter was a prime example. He could not have done much better than go to Charterhouse and Cambridge where he learned to play on very good pitches, and in that respect, I suppose, he was a prime product of top-class public-school and university cricket.

But I remember talking to George Geary, the former Leicestershire and England player who became the coach at Charterhouse, and congratulating him on what a great job he had done on Peter May as a schoolboy.

'I did nothing,' said George. 'He was such a marvellous, natural player that I could find very little fault in him from the first time I saw him play. I did give him a little bit of advice here and there but it was never a question of standing in a net and coaching him.'

Peter May played the game in a fairly simple manner. He would never hook and seldom pulled. And one very rarely saw him play a cut. He just hit the ball in an arc from cover point to mid-wicket, reducing his chances of error by cutting out those sort of shots where you are forced to play across the line. That was his great strength, and it was small wonder that in his capacity of chairman of selectors he almost despaired of the number of England batsmen who seemed incapable of playing straight.

He also hit the ball exceedingly hard, off both the front foot and the back foot, and was probably the finest on-driver the game has ever seen. On top of that, he played the game very hard, too. There was nothing soft about his cricket and he had no mercy on any bowler.

98

I never saw Peter play at school. But I did come across him playing for the Combined Services – he was a writer in the Navy – and I saw a fair amount of him when I did some coaching at Cambridge while he was up there. And I can tell you there was a great sigh of relief in the Oval dressing room when we discovered he was born in the adjoining county – or Minor County – of Berkshire which meant that he was automatically qualified to play for Surrey. It was the unanimous view of all the hard-bitten professionals in the Surrey side that, amateur or not, this guy would walk into our team – and be most welcome!

It is fair to say, I suppose, that David Ivon Gower probably had more of a natural flair for the game – and, perhaps, even more inborn talent – than P. B. H. May. But by the time he became England captain, David had in no way shown the same kind of ruthlessness, the killer instinct, that was such a feature of Peter's play.

Nobody can ever have timed the ball better than David Gower does. I will never forget the first time I saw him bat – in a John Player League match at Leicester on a wicket with no pace in it at all. The ball just was not coming on to the bat and several of the senior players I spoke to said it was obviously impossible to play strokes in such conditions. Then in came this blond, curly-haired 18-year-old at number four or five to stroke his first ball through the covers off the back foot for four and go on to time it as sweetly as though the ball was coming on fast and true. In my position in the commentary box, you sit up and take notice when you see anything like that, and it's the only time in the past ten years that any batsman has made that sort of impact on me.

It is such a pity that he has so far failed to fulfil his enormous potential through some strange lapses in concentration – made all the more annoying by the fact that he has shown himself capable of overcoming this weakness in pressure situations all round the world. In the West Indies, for instance, in 1981, only a fortnight after his twenty-fourth birthday, he batted through the last seven-and-threequarter hours for 154 not out to make sure of an honourable draw in the last Test in Kingston;

in Australia in 1982–3 he was easily England's most consistent batsman; and after a dismal tour of New Zealand in 1984, he went to Pakistan, took over the captaincy from the incapacitated Bob Willis and inspired a stricken side with 152 and 173 not out in successive Tests at Faisalabad and Lahore.

Those two innings suggested that his form would not be affected by the cares of captaincy – as Ian Botham's had been against the same intimidating West Indian opposition four years earlier. But then Gower went and let himself down again by getting out to two loose shots in his very first Test as captain in his own right and left everyone wondering whether the selectors had got the right man after all.

Personally, I thought it was the only sensible appointment, and I did not go along with the people who thought David was too happy-go-lucky (or laid-back, as I believe they say nowadays) to make a success of the job. I think that his outward appearance is deceptive and that he is extremely serious about his cricket. And one thing I am sure about. He is more annoyed than anybody about his lapses – because his face tells the story!

Another thing I am sure about, too. Gower's task on taking over the England captaincy was fifty times harder than May's was when he took over from Len Hutton in 1955. He went on to captain England a record 41 times and while I never considered him to be a great captain, he was certainly a very good one.

Strangely, in view of their totally different backgrounds, Peter had been a fervent admirer of Hutton throughout his career and I got the impression that he tried to captain England in a similar style to Leonard. That meant taking very few chances, and while there were many good reasons for Leonard to err on the side of caution, May was hardly in the same position. Hutton, after all, had never even captained Yorkshire. And as England's first professional captain there were a lot of people in high places looking for him to make mistakes. He just saw to it that he did not make too many!

May, on the other hand, had all the qualifications and

all the right credentials and could have afforded to be a bit more adventurous, though, from my own point of view, I got on much better with him that I had done with my fellow Yorkshireman. Hutton, for reasons which I have already explained, was obsessed with fast bowling whereas May tried to give everyone a fair crack of the whip.

Gower must envy them both the resources they had at their disposal.

Miller and Botham

In terms of statistics, Ian Botham is the most phenomenal all-rounder Test cricket has ever known. At the end of the 1984 season, he had scored 4,159 runs, including 13 centuries, and taken 302 wickets, including five or more in an innings 24 times, in 73 Test matches. Only two other cricketers have completed the double of 2,000 runs and 200 wickets in Test cricket. Sir Garfield Sobers scored 8,032 runs and took 235 wickets in 93 Tests; Richie Benaud had 2,201 runs and 248 wickets in 63 Tests. Among England all-rounders, only Tony Greig (3,599 runs and 141 wickets) and Trevor Bailey (2,290 runs and 132 wickets) stand anywhere near Botham's record.

Yet there are still plenty of people around who refuse to recognize Botham as one of the all-time great players. They point to the weakness of the opposition, especially Australia, at the start of his Test career which happened to coincide with the decimation of the Australian team by Kerry Packer; and they remember his alarming slump in form, which happened to coincide with his period as captain in two successive series against the West Indies, without question the best team in the world.

For my part, I must make it clear that Sobers was the greatest all-rounder I have ever seen, and am ever likely to see. But I rate Botham highly enough to compare him with the greatest of my generation and probably the greatest Australia has ever produced – Keith Miller.

Botham had nothing in common with either Sobers, the left-handed genius who could do anything on a cricket field with bat or ball, or Benaud, probably the last of the

101

great leg-break and googly bowlers. Nor was there much similarity between Botham and either the flamboyant, controversial Greig or the tough, unflappable Bailey. But the comparisons with the dashing Miller are endless.

Both Miller and Botham are cricketing cavaliers with an enormous zest for life. Miller was a pilot during the war; Botham is taking flying lessons in pursuit of an ambition to pilot himself around the world. Miller was a gambler, as familiar at Ascot or Epsom as he was at Lord's or the Oval; Botham knows his way round the racetracks too – and as an owner, at that. Both of them were irresponsible – yet take their cricket much more seriously than some people imagine. Both have powerful views on the game. And both were born to be colossal cricketers.

Their figures tend to suggest that Miller was the better batsman with 41 first-class centuries, seven of them double-hundreds, and Botham the more effective bowler. But in reality it is the other way round. Miller formed one of the most famous of all fast-bowling partnerships with the legendary Ray Lindwall while Botham is maturing as a batsman with each season that goes by.

Miller, to my mind, was a superb natural bowler. It seemed to come so easily to him that he did not even have to bother to mark out his run. He could simply set off from anywhere he liked without any apparent effect on the superb high action he retained until the day he finished playing. Nor did it interfere with his beautiful rhythm and uncanny accuracy which allied to the lift and movement he could extract from the deadest of wickets made him a bowler capable of destroying any side.

His great strength was his sheer unpredictability. He could bowl just about everything, and often did, sometimes to the extent of sending down six different kinds of delivery in the same over. He was so audacious that I remember him once letting David Sheppard have a googly in the first over with the new ball at Lord's – and getting him out with it! It was as cheeky as Botham playing that reverse sweep shot of his at a crucial stage of a Test match, though I don't think even Miller thought of that.

102

Botham, of course, also liked to experiment with his bowling, especially in his early days when it was at its best. He would bowl in-swingers and out-swingers, varying his pace and using the full width of the crease to change the angle of delivery. But the demands of one-day cricket have obviously had an adverse effect; and the fact that he has never been as lithe or loose-limbed as the athletic Miller may explain why he suddenly seemed to lose his ability to bowl the out-swinger.

He claimed he was as fit as he had ever been – thanks to his football training with Scunthorpe United – when he set off on the 1983–4 tour of New Zealand and Pakistan. But his bowling was still nowhere near as effective as it used to be and one can only hope that the cartilage operation, for which he returned home early, solved the problem.

In many ways, the 1984 season was seen as a crisis point in Botham's career, especially since he decided to take a break at the end of it and declared himself unavailable for the winter tour to India. But although he had already scored all those runs and taken all those wickets, it was important to bear in mind that at the start of the 1985 season he was still only 29 and should have plenty of good years in front of him. I have always believed that he is a lot better batsman than some people imagine and even though his bowling seems to be in decline his batting could still improve.

It was a lot easier for Miller to indulge himself as a batsman in a line-up that included Sidney Barnes, Arthur Morris, Lindsey Hassett, Neil Harvey and Don Bradman than it has been for Botham in an England side not known for its solidity. Miller probably had more shots, too, including the late cut which he played as well as anybody, but he never hit the ball as hard as Botham does. They say that Keith once put a ball over the roof at Lord's. But for sheer strength and consistency of hitting, Botham is miles ahead of him.

Finally, there is the question of captaincy. Underneath the extravagant exterior which Miller loved to present to the crowds was a very astute cricketing brain and Richie

Benaud, for one, has told me that Keith was one of the best captains he ever played under. Botham cherishes a dream of leading England again to prove to everyone – himself, included, one suspects – that he can make a far better job of it than he did last time. He could hardly do worse, but only time will tell.

Evans and Taylor

From 1946 until 1959, Godfrey Evans was an automatic choice as England's wicket-keeper and at his brilliant best he was the finest I ever saw. From 1967 until 1977, Alan Knott was considered similarly indispensable and that was only right because of the batting ability that supplemented his skill behind the stumps.

Yet day in, day out, Bob Taylor probably surpassed both of them as a pure wicket-keeper. While 'Godders' was the super showman and 'Knotty' an all-rounder extraordinary, good old Bob was the master craftsman.

It would be wrong to say that Evans's position was unchallenged. There were people around like my Surrey colleague Arthur McIntyre who was as consistently sound as anyone; Northants's Keith Andrew who was a superb keeper to both speed and spin; and Yorkshire's Don Brennan, a very classy performer, particularly to spin bowling, who kept wicket to me as well as anybody ever did. Where Godfrey had the edge was in the way he rose to the big occasion.

Evans probably had more off days than all the others I have mentioned put together. And he is probably still having nightmares about the most memorable of his off days – in the 1948 Test at Leeds. He must have missed half a dozen chances as Australia, set to score 404 in 345 minutes, won by seven wickets with 15 minutes to spare. Godfrey was very close to tears as he drove away from Headingley half an hour after the finish – something which must seem almost unbelievable to anyone who knows him as an irrepressible individual.

There were occasions when his sheer enthusiasm could get on your nerves in the dressing room, like the times when you needed about 400 to win and had slumped to

200 for seven and Godfrey was bustling around telling everybody that getting the runs was going to be a piece of cake. For all that, none of us was in any doubt that his brilliance often lifted the performance of the whole team, and especially of the bowlers.

He was at his best when keeping to Alec Bedser. A gambler on the field just as he has always been a gambler off it, Godfrey would always stand up to Alec, encouraging the bowler and intimidating the batsman in equal measure. And it was astonishing how many batsmen over-balanced trying to push away the late in-swinger, thereby giving Godfrey the chance to perform the kind of stumping the crowds love to see – on the legside by a wicket-keeper standing up to a quickish bowler.

The exceptional catches and stumpings that stick in the memory from that era invariably have the name of Godfrey Evans attached to them, so I suppose it was inevitable that when he returned to play for Kent his wicket-keeping often suffered a reaction. To go back to Dartford or some such place to play in front of 500 people was not really Godfrey's scene after all the glamour of a Test match.

That was the major difference between Evans and wicket-keepers like Knott and especially Taylor, who would approach a Test match against Australia in front of 90,000 people at the Melbourne Cricket Ground exactly the same as he would the last day of a county match in front of a handful of spectators at Ilkeston.

I first came across Bob Taylor when I was playing for Norton in the Staffordshire League. He was keeping wicket for a team called Bignall End, captained by my old England colleague John Ikin, and I well remember saying to him: 'Blimey, this kid's useful, isn't he?'

Ikin replied: 'His name's Taylor, and he won't be far short of playing for England before very long.'

He was not wrong. Yet Taylor was restricted to just one Test match – in New Zealand in 1971 – until Knott's defection to Kerry Packer's World Series Cricket finally gave him the opportunity to establish himself as England's no. 1 on the 1977–8 tour of Pakistan. By then,

Bob was a greying, 36-year-old who must have thought his chance would never come. But he took it as eagerly as he has taken any of his 1,400-plus catches in first-class cricket and despite several attempts by the selectors to find a younger man he was still going strong at the age of 43, when he was once again displaced by a superior batsman, this time Paul Downton. I always believed that Taylor just had the edge over Knott as a wicket-keeper, though there was never very much in it. But at the same time I always thought that Knott was the right choice. Apart from his exceptional ability as a wicket-keeper, he was capable of making some invaluable if unorthodox contributions with the bat – as more than 4,000 runs, five centuries and an average of 33.66 testify. It was only right and proper that he was picked for 95 Test matches.

But if ever a man deserved to play Test cricket it was Taylor. Wherever he has played – for Bignall End, Staffordshire, the Minor Counties, Derbyshire, England and various touring sides all round the world – he has always given of his best.

Great wicket-keepers are born not made. You can spot them at an early age by the way they take the ball into the gloves and by their movement behind the stumps as the feet go naturally into position. The wicket-keeper is the fulcrum of the game, the guy who has to keep everybody else on their toes. I cannot think of anyone who has done that job better – or in a nicer way – than Bob Taylor.

Benaud and Brearley

During this series of comparisons, I have touched on the subject of captaincy as it affected such great cricketers as Len Hutton and Geoff Boycott, Ian Botham and Bob Willis, Peter May and David Gower. And they all tended to prove the general rule that it takes a great side to make a great captain.

But there are exceptions. Richie Benaud, the greatest Test captain I ever came across, made an average Australian side into a very good one. And when Mike Brearley, the most effective England captain I have seen,

106

returned in 1981, he worked wonders with a side that had to be considered below average.

I have always maintained that Stuart Surridge was the best captain I ever played under, though he did have a quite exceptional Surrey side at his command. So one had to marvel at the achievement of Benaud who took over the Australian captaincy when Ian Craig, their youngest-ever skipper, fell ill, and led them to victory in four successive series, starting with a 4-0 triumph against England in 1958–9.

Looking back, it is hard to believe now that Benaud's appointment came as something of a surprise since most people had thought that Neil Harvey would get the job. As things turned out, he was a revelation. I never actually played with him but I am told by people who did – not just Australians but many others, including Englishmen, who took part in various tours under him – that he was a quite superb leader.

Having been closely associated with him for many years now as a television commentator, I know that Richie is a great stickler for detail. He likes everything to be just right, spot on. That is the way he runs his life, and that is the way he ran his cricket. He had everything worked out, including the opposition on whom he did his home-work so that he had a mental book on all the batsmen and bowlers.

Playing against him, one had the impression that he was alive the whole time, whether he was changing his bowlers, moving his fielders or switching his batting order. And like all the best captains he had the happy knack of being able to deal with different individuals in different ways, knowing which players needed encouragement and which ones needed the hard word. I would not say he was a brilliant judge of wickets but he did not make a lot of mistakes when he was putting the opposition in. He put them in an awful lot of times with an awful lot of success.

On top of all that, he was an inspiration himself. He developed into just about the best spin bowler in the world and with batting explosive enough to bring him the third fastest century in Test history he became the only Australian to take 200 wickets and score 2,000 runs in Tests. And added to his 248 wickets and 2,201 runs were 65 catches – another Australian record proving the magnificent example he set in the field.

Richie had courage, too, as he proved in one of his most memorable performances at Old Trafford in 1961. He was still suffering from fibrositis in his right shoulder which had prevented him from playing at Lord's when England were set to score 256 in little over even time to go 2-1 up in the series. We had reached 150 for one, thanks to a superb 76 in 84 minutes by Ted Dexter, when Benaud, knowing that the Ashes were at stake, took the ball. Bowling round the wicket into the rough, he dismissed Dexter, May, Brian Close and Raman Subba Row in five overs, finished with six for 70, saved the Ashes for Australia and brought his playing career to a perfect climax.

It came as no surprise to anybody that he went on to make such a success of his career in writing and broadcasting where his observations are always shrewd and well worked out – and invariably correct.

So what of the England captains I played under? Well, it will probably surprise many people to learn that the one who impressed me most was Norman Yardley who led England to a 3-0 victory over South Africa in 1947 but then had the misfortune to come up against Don Bradman's Australians in 1948 (losing 4–0) and John Goddard's West Indians in 1950 (losing 3-1).

I played in only three Test matches under Yardley but they were enough to convince me that he was a far better captain then he was given credit for. Bearing in mind that in 1948 he was in almost as hopeless a position as David Gower found himself against the West Indies in 1984, I thought Yardley did very well. He was a man you could listen to and learn from, and he was probably the best judge of a wicket I ever met.

But I have to admit that the best England captain I have seen was Brearley, a real mastermind whose recall in 1981 inspired Ian Botham and Bob Willis to such extraordinary heights that England won three successive Test matches against Australia to save the Ashes. Poor Kim Hughes, the Australian captain, must have wondered what had hit him when he suddenly found himself confronted by a grey-haired philosopher with all the qualifications that go towards making a good cricket captain, plus the most formidable brain that has ever been applied to the problem of winning Test matches.

You never want an idiot captaining a side, of course, and the better the brain the better you are going to do. But Brearley was also into psycho-analysis, and when he applied that kind of specialist knowledge to the handling of his players, the results were absolutely staggering, none more so than in the third Test at Headingley. With Australia needing only 130 to win, he first deprived Willis of the new ball, then put him on up the hill and into the wind. Only when his leading fast bowler was thoroughly browned off did Brearley let him loose at the other end — and Willis responded with a match-winning eight for 43, the best figures of his Test career.

It was indeed heady stuff, and total justification of the policy of picking a captain who many felt was not worth his place in the side. I never believed he was worth his place as a batsman because I did not think he was a player of Test class. But there are other aspects of the complex game of cricket that have always got to be taken into consideration, and Brearley's unique style of captaincy was one of them.

7

Characters of Cricket

I am not, as I hope you will have gathered by now, one of those old cricketers who is constantly harking back to the 'good old days', but in one respect the game is definitely not what it used to be. I would not go so far as to say that today's cricketers do not enjoy themselves because I do not believe you can play cricket at any time at any level unless you enjoy it. But they certainly do not seem to get as much fun out of it as we did. There are simply not the same kind of characters around these days. In recent years, the only real comedians I have seen are the irrepressible Derek Randall and the whimsical Ray East, and every time I look at them I think they should have been playing 20 or 30 years ago. They would have been in splendid company.

The first great character I met was Emmott Robinson, who gave me a lot of help when I was a boy in Yorkshire. There must be a thousand stories about Emmott whose all-round talent was not recognized until he was 35 but then kept him in the side until he was 47. The most famous of them has been told many times, but it is such a classic that I make no apology for repeating it here.

Emmott was bowling in a match against the university at Cambridge when an immaculately turned-out undergraduate came in to bat at no. 6. It took him ages to take guard and even longer to take a careful, studied look around the field. Then Emmott, who bowled little outswingers, ran up and bowled him one that ducked in, pitched about leg stump, moved away off the wicket and hit the top of the off stump.

For a moment, the undergraduate was absolutely speechless as he gaped back down the wicket. Then, remembering his upbringing, he had the presence of mind to say: 'Well bowled, Robinson, well bowled'.

'Ay,' said old Emmott, turning towards him, 'and it were bloody well wasted on thee.'

It was Emmott, of course, who is said to have told the great Neville Cardus: 'Ah reckon tha med me up'. And my other favourite story about him concerns a chance meeting between the two of them one cold, wintry morning in Market Street, Bradford.

The previous summer, Yorkshire had got into a lot of trouble in one of those bitterly-fought Roses matches before the war and they were looking to Emmott to play one of his great, match-saving innings on the last day. He was obviously determined to hold Lancashire at bay all day and at lunch had been in about two hours for nine. He was still there halfway through the afternoon on about 25 when, to everyone's utter amazement, he suddenly played a late cut. Old Emmott had never played a late cut in his life for the simple reason that the very thought of doing it had never entered his head. Now he set off for a run before he realized the full enormity of what he had done, stopped absolutely petrified in the middle of the pitch and was stranded as the guy at third man picked up the ball, whipped it in and ran him out. The last two wickets fell quickly and Lancashire won the match.

The following February Cardus was walking down Market Street when he saw the hunched figure of Emmott Robinson, hands stuffed deep into his pockets, flat cap pulled low over his downcast eyes, coming towards him. He did not notice Cardus until Neville greeted him: 'Hello, Emmott, how are you? Are you wintering well?'

Emmott looked up and recognized the speaker. Then there was almost a minute's silence before he said mournfully: 'Ee, Mr Cardus, I never should have done it, I never should have done it.'

I had a letter from Emmott when I was in Egypt during the war – and I am sorry to this day that I did not keep it. It was over three pages long but there was not a single punctuation mark, just one sentence that rambled on and on bemoaning the fact that there was no cricket because 'Hitler has buggered the whole thing up'.

If Emmott was the first great character I ever met, then the second was undoubtedly Stan Squires who was playing for Surrey when I joined them in 1946. He was still in his prime when he was taken ill with leukaemia and died within a few weeks at the age of 41.

Stan was a born humorist and certainly one of the funniest fellows I ever played with. Those were the days when we were not allowed to travel by car and all our trips to away matches were on the train. Stan always took his ukelele with him and would make up little songs and ditties to keep us amused on the way. Week in, week out, he would often have us in fits of laughter and though some of his more hilarious offerings may not be suitable for publication I can let you have a little of the taste with this extract concerning a former Surrey captain, who had better remain anonymous.

He stands there at cover
He stands oh so deep
That the batsmen run singles
Whilst he is asleep
And if he comes closer
It's still just a farce
'Cos he runs like a duck
With an egg up its arse.

Then there is the lilting little lyric he used to croon to keep his spirits up in the dressing room when the Surrey batsmen were engaged in some impossible run chase.

Throw your wickets away, away
Throw your wickets away
I don't care what becomes of me
As long as I hit out with my B-A-T
So throw your wickets away, away
Throw your wickets away
Sing of joy, sing of bliss
For the bowling is P---
And throw your wickets away.

112

Another comedian was Alf Barlow, a little guy who kept wicket for Lancashire in the early fifties but spent most of his winters going round the pubs and clubs in Manchester doing his 'turns'. He may not have been the greatest wicket-keeper Lancashire have ever produced and never became a household name as a comic, either, but he was full value on the Commonwealth tour to India in 1951. It is always important to have a humorist on a tour like that and Alf kept us smiling with turns like this:

Send out the MCC to India
Send out your bowlers and your bats
Send out your gallant wicket-keepers
And don't forget to take your spurs and spats.
Send out the boys of the MCC
Who made old England's name
Send our Sir Pelham, Rait-Kerr and Gubby Allen
But for God's sake don't send ME!

Around the same time, there was Charlie Harris, who opened the batting for Nottinghamshire with Walter Keeton and has to be one of the funniest men who ever played the game. I will never forget the first time David Fletcher came across him. He was making his debut for Surrey at Nottingham and before the match Charlie – well aware that the newcomer had never been to Trent Bridge in his life – dressed himself up in a pin-striped suit and a bowler hat complete with brief case and umbrella and introduced himself to David as the cricket writer of the local paper. Then he sat with him in the dressing room for half an hour taking down copious notes about his background, education, career so far, the lot. Within minutes of the interview coming to an end, 'Fletch' was flabbergasted to discover that his interviewer had quickly changed into his cricket clothes and was taking the field with the rest of the Nottinghamshire team. To his eternal credit, the shock did not stop David from scoring about 190!

Another Harris classic came at Trent Bridge during Nottinghamshire's traditional Whitsun fixture against Surrey in the days when the gates would have to be closed on both the Saturday and the Monday. I went in to bat about five o'clock with around 400 on the board and had scored a dozen or so when the second new ball became due. Harold Butler was taking it and as he walked back to his mark at the pavilion end I looked round to see he had three slips and two gullies – as was the usual case when I came up against the new ball! There was a hush as Harold began his run, but he had not got halfway to the crease when the silence was broken by a shout from one of the gullies.

'Hold it a minute, Harold,' cried Charlie Harris. 'Hold it up! I'm not ready.'

Harold stopped in his tracks. I looked round to see what was going on. And Charlie explained: 'Jim, lad, I think it's only fair to tell you. Unbeknown to you, he's put another gully in.'

I stared in amazement because I could not see any difference in the field, until I suddenly noticed, lying on the ground beside Harris, a complete set of false teeth grinning back at me. It was a typical Harris prank.

One of his favourite targets was Freddie Brown, who played for Surrey before he went to Northamptonshire. Charlie would delight in nominating every ball that Freddie bowled, calling out just as his arm came over 'leg break!' or 'googly!' before proceeding to play each delivery with the utmost relish.

It was the kind of humour that you don't come across in cricket nowadays, and another of the same vintage was George Cox who played for Sussex for the best part of 30 years. His father did the same so there had always been a Cox in the Sussex side from the turn of the century. And when George produced a son he was terribly ambitious that he would follow on and keep the tradition going. But the lad, unfortunately, had no interest in cricket whatsoever. He was a very bright boy who won a scholarship to Cambridge and obtained a degree there, yet for years George remained very upset about it all. He used to say that when the boy was naughty, he would punish him by taking him to a county match; if he was very naughty, he would take him to a Test match; and if he was very, very naughty, he would take him anywhere to watch Trevor Bailey bat!

I remember playing for Surrey at Hove one day when Cox came in to bat and got to about 30. I was in the middle of an over when he suddenly put his hand in his pocket, pulled out an enormous false moustache and clipped it under his nose. He was standing there like Aubrey Faulkner or somebody from the 1920s, but I did not notice the change in his appearance until I got to the point of delivery. Then I nearly died as a slow full toss slipped out of my hand, and he hit it straight over the pavilion for six.

George was also a good soccer player and his proudest boast was that he was understudy to Ted Drake at Arsenal, which meant that if Drake did not play, the forward line read: Hulme, Jack, Cox, James and Bastin. Actually George only played two or three times for the first team but he turned out regularly for the reserves and a clash between football and cricket fixtures produced a story that went round the county dressing rooms.

Sussex were due to play at Northampton and the side travelled north without George who was playing football and would not be joining them until later in the evening. They arrived at the Angel Hotel and captain Hugh Bartlett went up to the receptionist and announced: 'We are the Sussex cricket team.'

'Ah, yes,' said the girl. 'Very good. How many of you are there?'

'At the moment', replied Bartlett, 'there are ten of us . . . without Cox.'

At which point, so the story goes, the receptionist fainted.

John Warr, captain of Middlesex for years, was one of the game's great humorists and is still in huge demand as an after-dinner speaker. He had a quip for every occasion, such as the time we were playing Middlesex at Lord's in light far worse than they would ever contemplate playing cricket in these days. Appeals against the light were not allowed and when Warr bowled two quickish balls outside the off stump against Stuart

Surridge, our captain stared back down the pitch and said: 'Can't see a bloody thing, can't see a bloody thing out here'.

Two balls later, Surridge played and missed and over went his off stump. 'Couldn't see a bloody thing,' he grumbled as he made his way back to the pavilion.

'All right, Stuart,' said Warr. 'At least you've proved your point.'

My favourite example of the Warr wit came on the occasion of Bill Edrich's wedding – his fourth, I think. Admission to the reception was by invitation only and when Warr arrived without the necessary card the man on the door said: 'Sorry, sir, you can't come in here without a ticket'.

'Ticket?' exclaimed Warr. 'I've got a season ticket for these.'

I am not sure whether Johnny Wardle has ever had as much of a sense of humour off the field as he had on it, but when it came to the kind of antics that leave the crowd in fits of laughter he was the funniest man I ever saw. He had so many tricks which he performed with perfect timing, such as the stunt he pulled on an unsuspecting young West Indian batsman during England's tour of the Caribbean in 1954.

We were playing a minor match on a matting wicket on one of the smaller islands when drinks were brought out. The batsman discarded his bat and gloves and left them by the crease while he went in need of much-needed refreshment, whereupon Wardle stole up to the wicket and, with a dramatic flourish for the benefit of the crowd, shoved the bat under the mat. The batsman had seen none of this and when he looked for his bat he was immediately suspicious of Wardle, whose huddled figure as he retreated towards the boundary gave every indication that he had something concealed beneath his shirt.

The batsman gave chase to apprehend the 'thief', and the little ground almost shook with laughter when Wardle, now a picture of innocence, turned round and solemnly shook his hand while excited spectators screamed: 'Under de mat, man, under de mat!'

That was typical of Wardle's humour. And equally typical of the man was Colin Ingleby-McKenzie's remark when he was asked for the secret of his success in leading Hampshire to their first County Championship for 66 years in 1961. Discipline was the key, he said in all seriousness. He insisted that every member of the side was in by breakfast-time. . .

And it is a breakfast-time story that reveals the true nature of 'Ingers' who brought life and excitement to Hampshire cricket but whose greatest love in life was racing. Around that time, there were no two more contrasting characters in any county side than the fun-loving Ingleby-McKenzie and the Hampshire opening batsman Henry Horton, who was a very solid, staid performer. All cricketers devour the morning papers over breakfast, principally to see what has been written about themselves but also to find out how their competitors are getting on. And on the morning of one away match, Ingers came down for breakfast, late as usual, to find Henry still poring over the previous day's scorecards.

'I see Leicester won yesterday,' he said as his captain sat down at the table.

'And about time, too', retorted Ingleby-McKenzie. 'He hasn't been in the frame for two weeks.'

No chapter concerning the characters of cricket would be complete without mentioning Fred Trueman – though I have always believed that half the stories one hears about him are either untrue or, at the very least, wildly exaggerated.

But I do like the one Peter Parfitt tells about his own first appearance against Trueman at Lord's. All the Middlesex players were out on the balcony as Parfitt, trembling with apprehension, made his way out to the middle. Trueman was already pawing the ground at the end of his run, which stretched almost all the way back to the pavilion. And he completely ignored the incoming batsman who gave him a nervous glance on his way past.

Instead Fred looked up towards the home players' balcony just above him. 'All right,' he called. 'You can run his bath now.' And, sure enough, after softening up

the newcomer with one or two venomous deliveries, he
sent the petrified Parfitt packing for his early bath.

My own particular Trueman tale – which I know to be
true – again goes back to the West Indies in 1954. After
being unmercifully hammered in 1948, we had gone back
to the Caribbean with what we thought was a very strong
side – including Hutton, Compton, May, Graveney,
Trueman, Statham, Bailey, Lock, Wardle and myself –
but we found ourselves 2-1 down by the time we went to
Trinidad for what was the last Test match ever played
on a jute matting wicket.

The West Indies won the toss and made 681 for eight
declared with Weekes scoring 206 and Worrell and
Walcott a hundred apiece on a surface that was absolutely
perfect for batting. It meant we had to make 532 to save
the follow-on, which we managed to do, but not before
Fred and I had found ourselves facing the third new ball.

It was in the hands of a chap called Frank King from
Barbados, who, after about two days in the field, was still
bowling at something like 95 miles per hour, and Frank
Worrell, who, after a fairly long bowl in the heat, had
been reduced to something around my pace. As soon as
Fred came in, he called me down the wicket for a conference, only on this occasion it was not so much a conversation as a monologue since I took no part whatsoever.
Fred simply looked at King and he looked at Worrell and
then he said to me: 'I'll tell you what, Jim lad, thee take
King and I'll look after Worrell'.

In fairness to Fred, I must say I thought it was a
reasonable assessment of the situation – until about the
third delivery with the new ball. You could always tell
when King was going to bowl you a bouncer because he
ran up a bit quicker and you could see the whites of his
eyes, so, knowing what was coming, I went to hook it.
Unfortunately for me, though, the ball hit the seam of the
matting wicket, deviated and hit me smack over the right
eye.

Down I went with a huge gash on my head and blood
spurting out all over the place. There was no assistance
forthcoming from Fred, who had suddenly lost all his sun

tan and had no great desire to leave his end. So, with nobody else coming near me, I hauled myself to my feet, applied a handkerchief to the wound and set off groggily back to the dressing room for treatment.

It was only when I was passing Fred that he broke his silence. 'Bad luck, mate,' he said. 'But I thought I worked that out just about right.'

There were characters among the umpires too, and none greater than Alex Skelding who was responsible for that marvellous piece of poetry called 'The Umpire's Lament'. There was never any shortage of humour when he was standing in a match. He kept the game going and he kept it lively, although his patience was sorely tried during a varsity match in the fifties.

It was a long, hot day with the cricket slower than any Test match and when a well-bred undergraduate acting as twelfth man came out with the drinks halfway through the afternoon, he made quite a fuss of old Alex.

'Now then, Mr Skelding,' he said. 'What would you like to drink? We've got lemonade, ginger beer, or something stronger if you prefer it.'

'All I'd like', said Alex testily, 'is a glass of McLean's stomach powder because this cricket's giving me the bellyache.'

It was Alex, of course, who used to take the bails off at the end of each day's play and announce: 'And that, gentlemen, concludes the entertainment for today!' And though he did get the bellyache on the odd occasion, I am sure he and everyone else involved in the game did find it far more entertaining than they would do today.

8

Saddened by Yorkshire

The best thing that ever happened to me was to be born a Yorkshireman. I have always maintained that and always will, despite the fact that I never achieved every Yorkshireman's ambition of playing cricket for the county of his birth. I have no regrets about that for the simple reason that I was extremely lucky to get the opportunity to play for Surrey at a time when they were building the side that was to win the County Championship seven years in succession between 1952 and 1958.

It was Yorkshire, of course, who broke that sequence in 1959, and went on to win the title six more times themselves in the sixties. But what has happened to them since their last championship triumph in 1968 has saddened every Yorkshireman, and should have saddened everybody with the game of cricket at heart. And the saddest thing about it all is that their decline came as no surprise to those of us who had bothered to examine the roots, indeed the grass roots, of the problem.

Before I go into that, though, let me correct a popular misconception. It was written thousands of times during my career that Yorkshire let me slip through their fingers. But it was never true. They just did not think I was good enough to play for them, and, at the time they made that decision, I am sure they were right.

I was no different from any other lad born and raised in Yorkshire in that I dreamed of being a professional cricketer from the time I was old enough to hold a bat. And long before I left school I had two distinct objectives – first to play in the Bradford League and then to go on and play for Yorkshire County Cricket Club. But I only got halfway to fulfilling my ambition.

Saltaire thought enough of my ability to pitch me into their Bradford League side at the age of 16, and Yorkshire were sufficiently impressed to invite me to the pre-season nets at Headingley. Somewhere among my souvenirs, I have still got the postcard, signed by county secretary Jack Nash, offering to pay me ten shillings a day plus the tram fare for my attendance. It was my first professional contract, and for a long time afterwards I thought it was going to be my last! There were about 70 Yorkshire colts on parade and just as soon as the coaches began to put us through our paces I realised that at least 30 or 40 of them were far better players than I was. Some of them – notably Harry Halliday, who had already made a name for himself as a schoolboy prodigy and was in the Yorkshire first XI at 18, Willie Watson, Vic Wilson, Ken Fiddling and John Lawrence – were obviously in an altogether different class from me. And while I fully appreciated and indeed enjoyed the experience of rubbing shoulders with such talented young batsmen and bowlers, I went away convinced that I would never ever be good enough to play for Yorkshire.

At the time, I was no great shakes as a cricketer. I was a pretty ordinary, medium-paced bowler who could bat a bit, and that is how Yorkshire would have remembered me in 1946 when Surrey approached them for permission to sign me on special registration. Yorkshire had no objection. And I have to admit that if I had been a member of their cricket committee, I would not have had any objection either.

It must have come as a terrible shock to them when I first went back to Bradford to play for Surrey against Yorkshire, and they discovered that the modest, medium-paced trundler had turned into a genuine off-spinner bowling round the wicket. And goodness knows how they felt in 1950 when I had figures of 14 overs 12 maidens 2 runs 8 wickets in the Test trial, again at Bradford of all places!

I was still eligible to play for Yorkshire, of course, and

121

in the early fifties they paid me what was probably a unique compliment when I became the first and, I believe, the only 'exile' ever to be asked to go back and play for the county. Len Hutton had often asked me why I did not play for Yorkshire – he still does, come to that! – and it was on his advice that the then chairman came to see me during a championship match at the Oval and asked if I would consider going back. I had no hesitation in giving him a categorical 'No'. My attitude was simple enough. Yorkshire had agreed to release me. Surrey had given me an opportunity. I was quite happy where I was. Thank you very much.

That decision, I suppose, could have given rise to a degree of bitterness. But I have never quite been able to understand why I have always felt an air of tension whenever I have gone back to Yorkshire since then. It has never worried me too much. In fact the Yorkshire fixture was the one I most looked forward to every season. The crowd always treated me magnificently, yet for some reason that I have never been able to put my finger on there has invariably seemed to be a strange feeling of unease among the committee men. It still exists today for while I have been in the committee room once or twice for drinks with friends, I have never been invited there officially.

There has certainly never been any bitterness on my part, even when they did not want me all those years ago. You never lose your heritage. And I have always insisted that I learned more about cricket during my formative years in Yorkshire than I could possibly have done anywhere else. For one thing, cricket seemed to be the only topic of conversation and I believe you can very often learn as much about the game from talking to knowledgeable people as you can from spending hour after hour in the nets. But more important than that were those three seasons I spent playing for Saltaire in the Bradford League between the ages of 16 and 18.

Whenever I have watched club cricket in the south of the country, I have often been struck by the older players' benevolent attitude towards the younger ones. They tend to look much more kindly on a boy coming in to bat than they do in the tough, competitive atmosphere of the Bradford League. If I went in to bat and the opposition professional was bowling, he saw me as the chance of a cheap wicket and the cash collection he was looking forward to; if I was bowling, he would be looking to seize the opportunity of scoring some easy runs towards the half-century that would put a few more bob in the kitty. In that kind of cricket, you have to battle to survive, and that has never done anybody any harm.

In fact I would go so far as to say that an 18-year-old cricketer brought up in Yorkshire is as seasoned as a 22-year-old raised in the south. And I am convinced that those competitive northern leagues still contain the raw material to make Yorkshire as great as they ever were.

It is too easy to heap all the blame for their decline in recent years on to the committee, though they must obviously accept their share of the responsibility. It is too easy to blame everything on the overpowering influence of Geoff Boycott and, in the past few years, his personality clash with manager Ray Illingworth. And it is too easy to blame everything on the fact that Yorkshire are the only county who have not benefited enormously from the introduction of overseas players. For I am convinced that Yorkshire have no need to look outside their own county borders for their players, never mind overseas.

When I first started to watch Yorkshire before the war there were at least eight outstanding cricketers in their first XI – men like Herbert Sutcliffe, Len Hutton, Hedley Verity, Maurice Leyland, Bill Bowes, Arthur Mitchell, Wilf Barber and Arthur Wood. After the war, they still had a solid backbone of international cricketers – Hutton still, Fred Trueman, John Wardle, Bob Appleyard, Willie Watson, Vic Wilson, Frank Lowson and Brian Close. And when they last won the County Championship in 1968, they retained a nucleus of Test players – Close and Trueman, Geoff Boycott, Ray Illingworth, Phil Sharpe and Don Wilson.

But in recent years they have been reduced to just one player of true international stature – G. Boycott. And there must be some deep-rooted reason for that because enthusiasm for the game of cricket in Yorkshire has certainly not diminished.

The answer, I am sure, lies in the leagues since that is where every single one of the great names from the past learned his cricket. But that was in the days before the arrival of sponsors and with them, of course, the limited-overs game. Then, matches began at 2 p.m. and finished at 8 p.m.; there was no restriction on the number of overs a bowler could bowl or the length of time a batsman could bat; and every league side would contain a slow left-arm spinner who was given every opportunity to develop his skills.

Now limited-overs cricket in the first-class game has proved an outstanding success. Indeed, from the financial point of view it has been a lifeline for many of the counties. But I don't think the same can be said about its introduction to league cricket. They don't get many spectators anyway so crowd appeal does not really come into it. And the restrictions have made spin bowlers almost extinct, produced flaws in batsmen's techniques and reared a whole generation of defensive, medium-paced, leg-stump bowlers.

This change, I am convinced, is the basic reason for the lack of top-class talent emerging in Yorkshire at the present time. And surely there is a very simple solution. In this day and age, not too many people work on Saturday mornings – even those people who have got a job to do – so it should be possible for the major leagues to switch to playing on an all-day basis. This would encourage batsmen to build their innings, resurrect a few spin bowlers and, most important of all in modern cricket, encourage the fast bowlers. If they did that, I am sure it would not be very long before Yorkshire were again producing the kind of players who would lead them back to the top.

It would help, of course, if there was a degree of co-operation between the leagues and the Yorkshire committee, but as I write they still seem to be too preoccupied with internal politics to concentrate their minds on the roots of their problem.

I have already said that the committee cannot be blamed for everything that has gone wrong at Yorkshire, but the massive upheaval that followed the amazing decision to refuse Boycott a contract to play in his own testimonial season was long overdue. Even they must have known by then that they were becoming one of the biggest jokes in the cricket business.

In recent years, they had managed to create as much controversy – and attract as much animosity from some quarters – as Peter Tatchell did when he stood as Labour candidate in the Bermondsey by-election or Arthur Scargill when he was masterminding the miners' confrontation with the Tory government. In fact when you saw some of the election papers that candidates for the Yorkshire committee sent out to their 'constituents' it was far more vicious than some of the real political stuff. With every area in the biggest county in England having to be represented, the committee is so big and unwieldy that it is hardly surprising they have so much difficulty reaching agreement.

Certainly some of their decisions over the years have left considerable doubts as to whether they were getting the right kind of people running the club. Just look at their record. They managed to sack Johnny Wardle, their best post-war spinner, handed out the same treatment to Brian Close, their best post-war captain, and capped it all by giving cards and money to Boycott, the most prolific batsman in Test history.

I first came across Geoffrey Boycott towards the end of my career in 1963 when I was playing for Essex and he came down to Clacton to play for Yorkshire. Strangely enough, there was another colt playing in that Yorkshire side and I have to confess that on first appearance I thought John Hampshire seemed to be the better player. Be that as it may, I have got to know Boycott pretty well in the 20 years since then and I must say that we have had a fairly amicable relationship. Personally, I have always found him very kind and courteous. And I know

he has always respected my opinion and listened attent-
ively to anything I have had to say, even on the several
occasions I have found it necessary to remonstrate with
him over something he has said or done.

At the same time, it would be foolish of me not to
recognize the faults that have provoked so much criticism
from players and officials alike just about everywhere he
has been in the cricket world. If you go to Australia or
New Zealand, India or Pakistan, Sri Lanka or the West
Indies, you will always find someone only too eager to
tell you a story about Boycott's unfortunate knack of
upsetting people.

But before accepting all those stories as gospel, before
joining the chorus of condemnation, perhaps we should
think a little more deeply about why Boycott arouses such
emotions. Basically he is a loner – and always has been.
He has been driven on by a burning ambition to succeed
in everything he does – and he still is. And if it has meant
upsetting a few people by trying to get what he wants in
his own way, he has remained remarkably unconcerned.
In a word, he is selfish.

Selfishness is not an uncommon characteristic among
cricketers. I have always believed in stressing that cricket
is a team game, but I have never had much doubt that
every time a batsman goes in to bat or a bowler comes
on to bowl, he is almost totally preoccupied with thoughts
of his own success. If such thoughts happen to coincide
with the needs of the team, all well and good. If they
don't, well, it's just too bad. Trouble occurs when that
kind of attitude is carried to such an excess that it becomes
an obsession. And this is probably the case with Boycott,
though no more so than with a few other players I have
come across over the years.

Boycott's obsession, however, gave Yorkshire the
chance to use his influence as an excuse for their lack of
success during the past decade. Their disaffection with
the man began during his seven years as captain in which
time they failed to win anything, although they did finish
second in the County Championship in 1975. It is fair to
say – and I think Boycott himself would agree – that for

all his great knowledge of the game, both technical and tactical, he was never going to be one of the great captains. But it is also fair to point out that throughout his period in charge, the Yorkshire side he led on to the field was one of the weakest in their history. I have great doubts whether the legendary Brian Sellers himself would have been able to achieve much more than Boycott did with the players at his disposal.

What was unfair, I felt, was the attitude some people took when there was a suggestion that Boycott might be a better bet as England's captain than Mike Brearley. There could not have been much doubt in most minds that Brearley was streets ahead as a captain and, quite rightly, he was given the job. Yet some sections of the media disgraced themselves, in my view, by using the issue to denigrate Boycott rather than to champion Brearley.

History now records that when Boycott was stripped of the Yorkshire captaincy there was no sign of any improvement, either under John Hampshire or under Chris Old, who both became so disillusioned that they were happy to quit the county and start enjoying their cricket again elsewhere. Finally manager Ray Illingworth took over the captaincy himself – at the age of 50 – but he could not wave a magic wand, and in 1983 Yorkshire finished bottom of the County Championship for the first time in their history.

It was at the end of that season that they made the astonishing decision to sack Boycott after he had scored 1,941 runs for them at an average of over 55 – and been granted a testimonial the following year. It is true that he had twice been admonished by Illingworth for slow scoring and no doubt Illy had a reasonable point. But to refuse to give a man a new contract because he did not make his runs quickly enough on a couple of occasions must have been unprecedented. If such action was to become the norm, there would be a few batsmen around the country shaking in their shoes, including one or two in the England side.

Not surprisingly, such treatment of a man who has

always aroused extreme passions in Yorkshire almost led to civil war. Yet surely all the furore could so easily have been avoided. All it needed was for two or three of the more knowledgeable members of the committee to have taken Boycott on one side, spelled out to him the facts of cricket life, however unpleasant they might have been for him, and allowed one of Yorkshire's most famous sons to leave the club with dignity.

'Look, Geoff,' they should have said, 'we are going to give you a testimonial to thank you for your immense service to the county over the past 21 years. You are now 43 years of age and we do have one or two younger players knocking on the door so we would like you to finish your career with Yorkshire at the end of your testimonial season.'

He would still not have taken too kindly to such a suggestion at first. But I am sure that, on reflection, he would have accepted it.

Instead of that, Boycott and his many supporters were in no mood to accept anything and, marshalled by his close allies on the committee, Sid Fielden and Reg Kirk, they stepped up a campaign that was eventually to give them control of the club. Yorkshire's winter of discontent was too much for two of their most prominent figures, president Norman Yardley and chairman Michael Crawford, who both decided that enough was enough. I was one of many Yorkshiremen – on both sides of the argument – who felt aggrieved at the loss of two such loyal servants of the club who, throughout the months of turmoil, had behaved with a great deal of fairness and composure.

Other illustrious names went too, though not voluntarily. The Boycott brigade, showing tremendous enthusiasm, ensured that they were represented in most of the 39 seats when the committee elections were held in March 1984, with Geoffrey himself standing as a candidate for the Wakefield area. But they seemed to have little chance of success in the apparently safe seats of Harrogate, Leeds and Craven where former captains

Ronnie Burnett and Billy Sutcliffe and no less a personality than Fred Trueman were firmly entrenched.

When the votes were finally counted, however, Burnett,
Sutcliffe and Trueman had all been deposed, the Boycott
group had established a very handsome majority on the
committee and the man himself was in the unique position
of occupying a seat of power as well as a place in the
team, since his reinstatement as a player had already
become a formality.

Manager Ray Illingworth, who had long campaigned
for Boycott's removal from the scene, obviously had to be
the next casualty, and again I was sad to see him go. He
had faced an unenviable task in trying to shape a
successful side from his limited playing staff with precious
little co-operation from the old Yorkshire training grounds
and nurseries. No one could have produced much better
results in the circumstances.

The departure of a man of Illingworth's knowledge and
experience had to be a loss to Yorkshire cricket and it
was hard to believe that he would be adequately replaced.
But his exit coincided with the return of a character of
even greater stature. Brian Close, supporting the old
regime in the face of the Boycott landslide, had been
elected for the Bradford area with a big majority, and if
the new masters thought they were going to have everything their own way in the future, then they soon
discovered otherwise.

Close had been a schoolboy prodigy, England's
youngest Test player at the age of 18, a fine, proud Yorkshire captain before he was unaccountably sacked, the
inspiration of Somerset's climb to a position of power in
county cricket, a successful England skipper and, at the
age of 45, the bravest of all opening batsmen against a
brutal assault by the West Indian fast bowlers.

He had been a Test selector, cricket commentator,
student of horse racing and confidante of trainers, driver
of fast cars, even, on occasion, a free-fall parachutist.
Anything that offered a challenge appealed to him, and
now he found himself facing probably his greatest chal-

lenge of all when he became chairman of the Yorkshire cricket committee.

In his favour was the simple fact that everybody loved 'Closey', a big man in every sense of the word with a huge personal following. Against that was the simple truth that if he opposed the new regime – or, to be more accurate, when, since nothing was more certain – he was bound to be outvoted. And that would put him in a situation which he would find hard to endure for very long . . . and sure enough he was gone inside a year.

So, at the start of the 1985 season, one still had grave doubts as to whether a lasting solution had been found to the deep-seated problems of Yorkshire cricket. And at the heart of them remained Geoffrey Boycott who was going to find himself under even greater pressure, both on and off the field.

One could only watch in fascination, and wonder where it would all end.

9

Suspicious of South Africa

While South Africa's whites enjoy one of the highest living standards in the world, one third of all its black children under the age of 14 are stunted in their growth because they do not get enough to eat.

While its health system for whites has pioneered heart transplant surgery, its system for blacks has a ratio of one doctor to every 174,000 people in some areas and an infant mortality rate 31 times higher than the white rate.

While the country generates 60 per cent of all the continent's electricity, some of it from nuclear energy, the only fuel source for most blacks is firewood.

It is reports such as this – published in the *Observer* newspaper – which always persuade me to think again every time I feel I am being swayed by 'freedom in sport' campaigners like the Conservative MP John Carlisle and my old England colleague Denis Compton in their attempts to get South Africa readmitted to Test cricket. For I simply do not believe that it is possible to have multi-racial cricket in what is quite obviously not a multi-racial society. And for all the fundamental changes that have undoubtedly taken place in the past few years, I am not at all convinced that they are any more than window-dressing for the benefit of the outside world rather than their own black and coloured sportsmen.

I have every sympathy for the white South African cricketers who are deprived of the opportunity to test their talent at the highest level. Indeed, one can only admire what a lot of the top players – principally Mike Procter, Graeme Pollock and Barry Richards – have done to try to bring about fully integrated cricket.

I also had some sympathy for the England cricketers – notably Geoff Boycott, Graham Gooch, John Lever and John Emburey – who found themselves banned from Test and international matches for three years after taking part in the 'rebel' tour of South Africa in 1982. I am certain that they, like many of the other English professionals who spend their winters playing and coaching out there, have done all they can to help to bring about integration.

Personally, I could not see how the Test and County Cricket Board at Lord's could justify keeping them out of the England side for playing in South Africa at the same time as their own selectors were picking two South Africans, Allan Lamb and Chris Smith, to play for England, and the Government, no less, was giving preferential treatment to a 17-year-old South African athlete, Zola Budd, so that she could run for Britain in the Olympic Games. None of it made any sense at all to me. If people like Lamb and Smith and even Miss Budd had wanted to settle in England as permanent residents, there might have been some justification for selecting them in our teams, but they were simply getting the best of both worlds by coming to England to pursue their careers because they were unable to do so in their own country. Meanwhile, there were surely grounds for some reduction in the sentences handed out to Boycott, Gooch and company. After all, even a criminal is entitled to remission.

Having said that, however, let me stress that I always felt the original bans were right. The 'rebels' were wrong to go to South Africa since their action was clearly a threat to the future of Test cricket, and the authorities had to take immediate steps to deter others who might have been tempted to follow them. The players involved were well aware of the risk they were taking. And, with the benefit of hindsight, many of them probably regret taking it, not just because of the effect it has had on their Test careers but also from the financial point of view.

I could understand the attraction. Apart from the chance of ready money, South Africa offers a fantastic experience to any cricketer. The climate is quite superb. The hospitality is the best in the world. There is tremendous enthusiasm for the game. And the brilliant organization means that the tourist is always shielded from the harsh reality of apartheid.

Not that I knew anything about that when I first set foot on South African soil in September 1941, on a tour that had nothing to do with cricket. I was on a troopship *en route* to the Middle East and after steaming round the Cape we were given a few days' break in Durban. It was the first time I had stepped ashore since leaving war-torn England with its bombing raids, black-outs, food rationing and all sorts of other restrictions, and Durban with the lights shining, the shops open and everything imaginable on sale obviously made a very deep impression on a lad of 19. So did the way everyone rushed to entertain the troops and I decided there and then that when the war was over I would be back to see more of South Africa at the first opportunity.

I was disappointed not to get it on the 1948–9 MCC tour led by George Mann because I had been to the West Indies the year before and felt I had done well enough to be selected again. But the selectors decided not to take an off-spin bowler and I had to wait until the following winter, when, with nothing planned at home, I took a coaching job in Durban and was there from September right through until April, working as hard as I have ever done in my life. I was coaching from nine in the morning until seven at night five days a week and playing on Saturdays and Sundays.

There were kids of all ages from primary schools up to the provincial colts side, including such outstanding prospects as Trevor Goddard, who was a pupil at Durban High School, and Hugh Tayfield, who learned his cricket as a Natal colt before eventually going up to Johannesburg. But every boy I coached had one thing in common. They were all white.

It was only when I was given a lengthy break over the

Christmas period that I encountered any blacks at all – and that was quite by accident. I had met a mines manager and his wife on the ship on the way out to South Africa and when I decided to spend some of the holiday in Johannesburg watching the Test match between South Africa and Australia they invited me to stay with them for a couple of days.

While I was there, my new-found friend – not an Afrikaaner but of English stock – mentioned that there were thousands of Africans working in the mines who were interested in cricket and wondered if I would be prepared to meet them and give them a bit of coaching. I was quite happy to do that and it turned out to be a fascinating experience, meeting about 50 blacks who were all natural athletes and tremendously keen but knew little or nothing about the game of cricket.

Only two or three of them would ever have made the grade. But there was one chap who had a fair idea about batting – apart from the fact that he did not have a clue about using his feet and just stood there, rooted to the spot, smashing the ball to all quarters of the field. I showed him how to go down the wicket and get to the pitch of the ball, and he picked that up so well that I had a letter a few months later saying that he had played in a local match and made a hundred, moving down the wicket to everything and hammering it out of sight!

The next step, of course, would have been to show someone with a basic concept of bowling what to do when a batsman came charging down the wicket at him, but I never got the chance to do that. And, quite frankly, I never gave it a thought at the time.

As a 27-year-old professional cricketer, I was not interested in politics and still knew nothing about apartheid. The main thing that struck me that winter was the enormous gap between South Africa and Australia, who completely dominated the series. They won four of the five Test matches, two of them by an innings, with the other one drawn. And Neil Harvey, with whom I was going to have some memorable duels, averaged 132.

It was much the same when I went back to South

134

Africa in 1956–7 as a member of Peter May's touring side. They were long tours in those days, leaving England by ship in September and not returning home until the end of March, so one got a chance to see a lot of the country. But we never saw anything of what life was really like for the vast majority of the population. We were looked after by whites, shown around by whites, entertained by whites. Few of us even spoke to a black South African the whole time we were there.

Once again, my view of a winter spent in South Africa was purely in cricket terms. And in that respect, the series was the worst I ever played in. It was ruined by the two Trevors – Bailey bowling defensively on one side and Goddard doing the same thing on the other. P. B. H. May, arguably England's greatest post-war batsman, averaged 15 in the five Tests. And just about the only thing that impressed me was the bowling of Johnny Wardle who took 90 wickets at 12 runs apiece on the tour.

My only other lasting memory is that I finished bottom of the tour bowling averages for the only time in my career, despite taking 50 wickets at 17.5. That gives an idea of the strength of the England bowling at the time – and also indicates that South Africa were not always as strong a side as some people would have you believe. Our impression at the end of that tour was that they had a very useful squad of about 14 or 15 players but then there was a marked deterioration in standards. With just five Tests to play and only Natal and Transvaal providing anything like demanding opposition in the provincial games, it added up to a fairly cushy tour, which probably explains why generations of cricketers look back on their trips to South Africa with such nostalgia!

I have only been back once since then, for a week in December 1965. But I learned more from that brief visit than I had done from all my previous trips put together. For it was the first time I had been able to see the other side of the picture and to experience first hand some of the horrors of the system of apartheid.

My invitation had come from the Cape Coloured

135

cricketers who wanted me to present some prizes and speak at a dinner in Cape Town. I was met at the airport by the sports editor of their own local newspaper, which was sponsoring the event. He was himself a Cape Coloured, though I would not have known it since he was almost as fair-skinned as I am.

Having just got off the plane, the first thing I wanted to know after the formal introductions was the way to the gents' toilet. He led me into the airport lounge, pointed to a door and said: 'You go in there, but I can't come in with you. I've got to go to another one.'

'You must be joking,' I said, giving him a sideways sort of look.

'No,' he said, 'I'm afraid I'm not joking. And if you are shocked at that, just wait until you see my son.'

And, sure enough, I was even more taken aback when I was introduced to the strapping, 6ft. 2in., blond-haired, white-skinned youngster who, like his father, was classified as 'coloured'.

I had gone for tea at the sports editor's hourse – a nice, little, detached bungalow – and I was interested to know how much it cost to live in the area, where I had never been before because it was wired off from the neighbouring district. 'Well, I'm on the edge of the demarcation line,' said my host. 'On the other side of the railway line is the 'whites' area. It costs something like £5,000 or £6,000 more for me to buy my house than it does for them to buy a similar one.'

There had been a few changes from the last time I had been in Cape Town. I stayed at the President Hotel and blinked the first time I saw that there were black people staying there. That would certainly not have been the case 17 years earlier. So there had been some progress.

But there were no signs of progress for the coloured cricketers, who are not accepted by the whites and not accepted by the blacks. I spent the whole week with them, watching their matches and witnessing the conditions under which they played. And, in truth, it was horrendous. There was no such thing as a turf wicket. They played on matting laid down on a rough field. A broken

136

down old shack served as a pavilion. Lunch was a hot pattie eaten standing in a corner. Tea was a bottle of orangeade sipped through a straw.

The Cape Coloureds have their own inter-provincial competition and the Western Province side were going to play Natal in Durban. But instead of taking a comfortable hour-long flight like their white counterparts would have done, they were going all the way in the back of a 15-hundredweight truck which was going to take them two days. And naturally they felt very bitter about the situation.

It was easy to understand why. For there were a lot of very promising young cricketers among them. Indeed, I would go so far as to say that you could have picked out another four or five Basil d'Oliveiras from the people I saw playing. But the only advice they ever got was from within their own ranks. No overseas coaches went near them. They had no hope, no chance at all.

South Africa's supporters tell us that the situation is better now. And since it is impossible to argue otherwise when one has not been there for almost 20 years I have to accept that some changes have taken place. But however well intentioned the cricket authorities might be, they still hit a tremendous barrier when they come up against the political situation in the country. And I just do not believe that it is ever going to change.

I had two invitations to go back to South Africa during the winter of 1983–4 but I turned them both down. I would not have been allowed the opportunity to see what was really happening behind the window-dressing, to find the answers to the vital questions. How far do the changes extend to the grass roots of black and coloured cricket? What kind of treatment do the children get? What kind of schools do they go to? What kind of opportunities do they have?

Until we get the right answers to those, my doubts and suspicions will remain. And I, for one, will stay away.

10

Gentlemen of the Press

I have lost count of the number of people who have envied me my way of life over the past 30 years. Many of them, naturally enough, are those people who spend most of their lives working in some job for which they have no great love and can hardly wait for the weekends to indulge their sporting fantasies or simply get away from it all by watching their particular counties. Others are prominent personalities in the worlds of business, commerce or the arts who have risen to the very top of their chosen professions. And it never ceases to amaze me how many of them would have sacrificed everything just for the chance to play in a Test match at Lord's or tour Australia as a member of the England team.

Personally, I always felt that if I had not been lucky enough to be endowed with sufficient skill to play the game at the highest level, the next best thing would certainly have been to write about it. So I consider myself doubly fortunate in that I was invited into the Press box as long ago as 1961 to cover all five Tests against Australia for the now defunct *Daily Sketch* and am still enjoying the company of the gentlemen of the Press in my work for the *Daily Express*.

It never occurred to me that I should ever talk about the game or be asked to commentate on live action and it was quite by chance that I drifted into television, which has suited me far better than radio would have done. There are no problems 'talking over' or 'filling in' for a few minutes on television but to keep going for such lengthy periods as the commentators do on radio has never really appealed to me. I do have the utmost admiration for those who can sustain the listeners' interest and in this respect John Arlott has had no peer. He remains for me our number one broadcaster.

With this sort of background – player, pressman and broadcaster – I feel I can claim some sort of authority to assess the varied contributions made by my colleagues in the media, though I appreciate that it means treading on a fairly slippery slope. Ever since the game began, there has been an element of distrust between players and Press, and most cricketers tend to avoid discussing the relationship for fairly obvious reasons.

Yet it seems to me that the rapport has improved greatly in recent years. And I have to smile when I hear some of the present-day England players – notably Bob Willis, Ian Botham and David Gower, none of whom seem to have had an awful lot to complain about – moaning about the treatment they have received from the media. They will never believe me, I know, but I can assure them that it was a lot more vicious in my day.

We hear a great deal of the word 'pressure' from today's leading sportsmen yet I find it hard to comprehend that there has been any more pressure on, say, Willis and Greg Chappell than there was on Len Hutton and Don Bradman. The Don, in particular, was never free from the attentions of the Press and at one time what he had for breakfast was considered to be a news items.

The enormous increase in radio and television coverage has obviously made extra demands of the players but it does not cause the same kind of aggravation as there was when there were so many more newspapers – and consequently pressmen – for ever on the look-out for any scrap of information. Most of the national dailies, including the *News Chronicle*, the *Daily Herald* and the *Sketch*, which all bit the dust in rapid succession along with several Sunday papers, employed not only a cricket correspondent but often a 'name' writer as well who had to have his 'ghost' with him. And London alone could boast three evenings, the *Standard*, the *News* and the *Star*.

So when we went to Australia in 1958, for instance, the

players were outnumbered by the Press by something like three to one . . . and you can well imagine what it was like spending three weeks at sea on board the *Iberia* surrounded by 40 or 50 newspapermen all under pressure from their offices to provide a different story every day. I well remember one of the London evening paper writers showing me a cable he had just received from his editor. It contained just two words: 'Remove digit'. In the circumstances, it was not surprising that there were a few incidents not conducive to good player–Press relations.

I had been tipped off about one particular Australian columnist – a certain Jim Mather – who had established quite a horrendous reputation among the England cricketers because of his slanderous 'scoops'. Apparently on one tour before the war, he so incensed many of the players that he was last seen being pursued down a single-track railway line by a murderous-looking posse led by Bill Voce before disappearing into the bush. They obviously failed to catch him – for when we arrived in Sydney, there was Jim waiting to greet us.

Yet I never had any problem with him. Whenever I had a bit of information – never sensational or scandalous but quite newsworthy all the same – I used to slip it to him and consequently he never plagued me. There were still the usual scandalous stories about late-night parties, drinking bouts and the rest which inevitably begin to appear when things are not going well on a tour, but one learned to live with those, and hope that the little lady 13,000 miles away would do the same. Even so, it was not difficult to envisage the situation on a miserable, bitterly cold February morning back home when the milkman, having just digested his morning papers, would treat her to a wry smile and words to the effect that at least the old man appeared to be enjoying himself in the sunshine.

Bob Willis's team got a taste of how bad it used to be on the 1983–4 tour of New Zealand and Pakistan which was soured by all kinds of wild allegations about sex orgies and pot-smoking, but they were the work of 'hard' newsmen and so-called investigative journalists and thankfully the days of the sensation-seeking cricket writers seem to have gone. And consequently relations between players and Press have become far more harmonious.

There has been a considerable change in the kind of people filling the Press box seats these days. When I was playing, the majority were journalists who had arrived in the traditional manner from the ranks of junior reporters on provincial newspapers, learning their trade the hard way before breaking into Fleet Street. Alex Bannister, Crawford White, Frank Rostron, Bill Bailey and Bruce Harris are names that spring to mind. Such people still form the backbone of the present-day correspondents, such as my own colleague Pat Gibson, Michael Carey, Peter Smith and Alan Lee, the last two having benefited, like several others, from early training at Reg Hayter's long-established London agency.

Alongside them are to be found a batch of former first-class cricketers who have taken up the pen after distinguished playing careers. Robin Marlar, Tony Lewis, Jack Bannister, Eric Hill and Tony Pawson are among them, though Richie Benaud and the late Jack Fingleton can not really be placed in that category since they were trained reporters before starting their cricket careers. Yet another grouping contains Peter Laker, John Thicknesse and Henry Blofeld, good cricketers who did not quite make the first-class scene before embarking on journalistic lives.

Finally, it is easy to recognize the old – or should I say former – Test cricketers who almost make up a team themselves as their number steadily grows. They supplement their incomes with frequent and sometimes highly critical observations, and not surprisingly the current players seem to take far more exception to their writings than some of the more bona fide journalists.

Yet nothing is more certain than that in the next decade we shall see the Willis's and the Gowers replacing the Truemans and the Comptons and they in turn will come in for the same kind of complaints. It all adds to the continuing debate about the game of cricket, probably better represented in the Press than any other sport.

Most reporters, if they are honest, will admit to having their own particular favourites on the cricket field, and I am no different from other cricketers who have their own particular favourites among the Press.

I mourned the passing of Neville Cardus – not that I ever had a high regard for his technical knowledge. Some of his writing was unforgettable and I know almost by heart his autobiography which includes the account of the last Roses encounter before the 1939–45 war. On the same pedestal as Cardus, I would place R. C. Robertson-Glasgow, John Arlott and Alan Ross for their books. Ross's *Cape Summer,* published back in 1957, is a classic.

For the day-to-day reporting of the game, I was always an E. W. Swanton fan. When it came to producing a fair and accurate account of a day's play, he did it better than anyone else, even though some of the old 'professionals' believed there was a certain bias in favour of the amateur. There is no doubt that there are distinct advantages in working for a paper like the *Daily Telegraph* which gives a massive amount of column space to cricket and allows its men to cover play in much greater detail. Many of their daily newspaper colleagues are allowed only seven or eight paragraphs in which they can only highlight the outstanding events and I am sure that several would have been much more highly rated had they worked for the *Telegraph, The Times* or the *Guardian.*

For many years, Alan Gibson has been a prolific writer and commentator, a man of great talent whose wit appeals to quite a cross-section of the community. And as a purely professional journalist, the late Brian Chapman was superb.

I first met Brian during the England tour of the West Indies in 1953 when he joined us because it seemed there might be some political problem in Georgetown. He had held senior editorial appointments in Fleet Street but had tired of being desk-bound and relished the freedom of a trip to the Caribbean. But he freely admitted that his knowledge of the game was infinitesimal and made it clear that any help would be appreciated. None of us had ever heard anything like that from a reporter before and the team took to him immediately.

He became a cricket convert and graced the Press box for the next 25 years. To watch him work was a revelation, to me at least. He would sit quietly for most of the day, just taking the odd note. Then, well into the last session, out would come the typewriter and, with scarcely a moment's hesitation, his copy was pounded out and phoned through and he was on his way almost before the players had finished their showers.

As a bowler of off-spinners, Robin Marlar was an enigma. On his day, he was in the very top flight and could consider himself most unlucky not to play for England. There were other days, though, that were best forgotten. And I cannot help thinking that in many ways his writing has followed a similar pattern. Blessed with a brilliant academic mind, he has produced some real masterpieces, but some of his theories I have found difficult even to follow never mind to understand. Still, I turn most readily to my *Sunday Times* each weekend.

It was for an entirely different reason that my old friend and colleague Alf Gover was for a long time the envy of all his colleagues in the Press. He held the position of cricket correspondent of the *Sunday Mirror* and throughout the summer he would either drive or take a Saturday morning train before settling down to write his Sunday feature without ever having the harrassment of such daily problems as deadlines, constant rewrites or difficult sub-editors. A winter tour almost amounted to a six-month paid holiday with a luxurious three- or four-week cruise to enjoy before settling down in Australia where he was only required to produce copy once a week. The story got around that he knew every grain of sand on Bondi Beach and eventually became an honorary member of the Beach Club!

On a sad note, I must mention two gentlemen of the Press who wrote their final paragraphs at an early age. Ron Roberts and Clive Taylor were held in the highest regard by the players as well as the whole of the media and both have been greatly missed. They made their contributions to the memorable phrases and sentences I have read over the years – though the author of the one that springs most readily to mind had better remain anonymous. One evening in 1950 after a hard day in the field against the West Indies at the Oval, I sank into a corner seat on the train home, unfolded my copy of the *Star* and read: 'Bedser finally clean bowled Weekes with a ball he should have left well alone'. I suppose it could have been a bad line between Kennington and the copy-taker.

More recently – and more amusing – was Michael Carey's description of Derek Pringle pulling a muscle while writing letters, though in the Essex all-rounder's defence I was a witness when Johnny Wardle damaged a cartilage while playing snooker and also missed a Test match.

Pat Gibson brought howls of delight to many dressing rooms when covering the Headingley Test between England and Pakistan in 1982. Poor Vic Marks was utterly perplexed facing the spin of Abdul Qadir who finally bowled him with a googly. 'I am not quite sure what Vic Marks was reading at Oxford,' wrote Pat, 'but it was certainly not leg-breaks and googlies.'

One aspect of cricket reporting which I am sure will surprise many current England players as much as it did me when I first encountered it is the 100 per cent loyalty to English cricket to be found in the Press box. Without exception, the English journalists are desperately anxious to see their side come out on top, and it is never more obvious than when we are doing well and there is a solid representation of overseas reporters present.

Their criticism of England teams when we are not doing so well can often be measured in terms of disappointment and I always felt that a good example of this was provided by the attitude of one of the most controversial characters ever to write about cricket, E. M. Wellings of the London *Evening News*. In his early days, 'Lyn' Wellings was a very useful cricketer, both at Oxford and, on occasions, with Surrey. No one could ever doubt his great knowledge of the game and few people were more in love with it than he was – though he may not have admitted it too often. The problem was he set standards for all our players possibly on too high a plane and if anyone fell short of those standards he could become both vicious and cynical. In Australia, he could not be described as England's most popular or diplomatic ambassador but the feeling was mutual and his most sleepless nights would occur when we were getting a hammering. Like all the players, I would come under the whip myself every now and again, yet for all that I have to say that I always found E. M. W. interesting and very readable.

It would probably be interesting to hear his views on another section of the media whose status seems to have grown dramatically in recent years – the scorers or, to be more exact, the statisticians. Gone are the days of the scorers pure and simple, treasuring their small, green-bound books. They have been overtaken by men with much more sophisticated methods, originated soon after the war by Arthur Wrigley, Jack Price and Roy Webber and developed to a highly professional level by Bill Frindall and Irving Rosenwater. It is strange that the first three named all died suddenly at an early age between 1962 and 1965 and the same fate befell Michael Fordham in 1982 when he was only 53. With Irving Rosenwater emigrating to Australia to join the Packer gold rush, the way was clear for Wendy Wimbush to become the first full-time professional lady scorer and add her name to the illustrious list.

Most of us on radio and television watched with amusement the intense rivalry that existed for several years between Frindall and Rosenwater on radio and television respectively. The enormous amount of detail pertaining to cricket statistics and the glut of Test matches these days means that records are going by the board almost every day and it became a battle royal as they tried to scoop one another.

As individuals, they are poles apart. Irving's profound knowledge of the game is largely based on hours of study, prolific reading and the most conscientious observation as a spectator. His playing career was of a limited nature, though he gives us all constant reminders of the slip catches he used to take off the bowling of Ken Higgs in Services cricket. But, more than anything, his biography of Sir Donald Bradman, skilfully researched, packed with detail and compiled almost as a labour of love, epitomizes the man. At the drop of a hat, he could supply some little-known fact about a certain player – yet the odds would be stacked heavily against him recognizing the same player should he suddenly appear in the commnetary box.

Bill Frindall is a completely different character who will go down in cricket history as the first person to make a profitable living from keeping the score. Hard-working, conscientious and very, very professional, he has probed the depths of the game's statistics as no man before him and for his industry alone he is deserving of his success. In a changing world, he has become almost as well known as the players who supply his needs.

One has to wonder, though, how valuable are the thousands of facts and figures so readily supplied by these diligent individuals. They must be extremely valuable to radio commentators who have so much time to fill, and on television too I must admit they do help to fill in some awkward moments, but with so many flying through the air on any given day it is vital to be able to sort out the relevant ones. Heaven forbid that one day we shall be told that David Gower has just made his 1,000th stop in the gully. On the other hand, it *is* of interest to learn that a certain batsman has been repeatedly caught by the wicket-keeper or first slip in his recent innings or that another batsman is repeatedly being adjudged lbw.

As for the records themselves, it is equally important to assess how much they really mean. For instance, Fred Trueman and Bob Willis have both exceeded 300 wickets in Test matches. But it took Fred 67 Tests to reach 307 wickets and Willis nearer 90 to overtake him. And if you look further back you will discover that the great Sydney Barnes took his 189 Test wickets at seven per match. At that rate, he would have collected 469 wickets in 67 Tests whilst in 90 his haul would have been no fewer than 630, or more than double Willis's striking rate!

146

Elsewhere in this book and in various other publications, I have discussed television coverage and the people involved. But I would like to say a word or two on behalf of our colleagues on the radio who have come in for some pretty harsh criticism from various quarters during the past year or so. They have been accused of falling standards yet that was only to be expected after the departure of John Arlott. The impact he had made for the best part of 40 years was immense and there was no way in which he could ever have been adequately replaced.

The critics suggest that the radio commentators get themselves involved in too many peripheral subjects rather than concentrating on the game itself and consider that few people are interested in lengthy chats about the state of health of Fred Trueman's dog or the quality of the latest batch of cream cakes. But I consider that they have a more exacting task than we do on television. And, quite frankly, I should like to hear some of the more strident critics keeping rigidly to the game itself throughout a six-hour day as four fast bowlers dawdle back 30 yards to deliver each ball.

Radio's team is led by Brian Johnston, the youngest 70-year-old in the business whose enthusiasm for the game has never wavered. He is a perfect example of the many people in the media who would willingly have sacrificed most things in life to have been a Test cricketer. One writer and broadcaster who was, of course, is Trevor Bailey who, in my view, stands head and shoulders above any other radio comments man. He is accurate to a degree in his assessments which are always concise and very much to the point, thereby giving a good balance to the programme.

Finally, no chapter on the media would be complete without a mention of the two leading photographers – Patrick Eagar and Adrian Murrell. It was Patrick who first brought a new dimension to cricket photography and with Adrian emulating him in recent years they have built up a library containing examples of their art which have enriched the game to an extent that the great players of the past could never possibly have dreamed of.

147

11

The Way Forward

There were the usual cries of 'Sack the lot of 'em!' after Bob Willis's England team had been ignominiously beaten by an innings and 132 runs in Christchurch and by three wickets in Karachi to lose both Test series on their 1983–4 tour of New Zealand and Pakistan. They were such pitiful performances that the after-match inquests went a lot further than the actual game of cricket with one Fleet Street newspaper sending a team of reporters – or 'investigative journalists' as they seem to call them nowadays – to the other side of the world to look into allegations of pot-smoking, excessive drinking and late-night parties.

Even if they were true, I doubt if the players' activities off the field would have had very much to do with England's performances on it. For the state of English cricket – indeed the state of world cricket – in the eighties means that results which would have been inconceivable not so many years ago are becoming commonplace. And there are perfectly valid reasons for the shift in the balance of power which has left the West Indies reigning supreme and very little to choose between the other Test-playing countries.

There is no doubt that when I first became deeply interested in the game before the 1939-45 war there was only one Test side in the same class as England, and that was Australia. It was unheard of for either India or New Zealand to beat England anywhere and though South Africa and the West Indies were a little stronger few people would ever have backed them to win a Test series in England.

The first sign of a major change came in 1950 when John Goddard brought over a West Indies team containing Weekes, Worrell and Walcott and those two little pals of theirs, Ramadhin and Valentine, and thrashed England by three Test matches to one.

The West Indies had always been a force in the Caribbean where England have won only two series – in 1959–60 under the captaincy of Peter May and in 1967–8 when Colin Cowdrey's side took advantage of a typically quixotic declaration by Gary Sobers to snatch a dramatic victory. But it was not until West Indian players began arriving in this country in large numbers that they began to develop into a team capable of winning anywhere in the world. With very few exceptions, all their Test players since then have benefited from playing League cricket in England. And when they were allowed into county cricket as well, their team took an even greater leap forward.

They have always been natural cricketers. It obviously helps to play the game with the sun on your back all the year round on an island like Barbados which has been responsible for producing so many of the West Indian world-beaters. I have been there many times and there is no doubt that cricket is a religion handed down from generation to generation. There is a little bit of soccer in the Caribbean; a few people play tennis; and horse racing satisfies the needs of those with a passion for gambling. But for most West Indians cricket is the only sport that matters. And there is nothing they like better than to see a chap bowling at 100 miles per hour. So if a youngster is lithe and athletic, as so many of them seem to be, there is every encouragement for him to become the next fast bowler to roll off the production line in succession to Andy Roberts and Michael Holding, Joel Garner and Malcolm Marshall and the rest.

Yet for all that natural talent and all their latent enthusiasm, there can be no doubt that it is the experience which so many of their players have gained in England which has made the West Indies well nigh invincible in

Test cricket. We used to call them 'calypso cricketers', but not any more. Under the captaincy of Clive Lloyd, who arrived in England to play League cricket for Haslingden in 1967 and joined Lancashire a year later, they have developed into a ruthlessly professional, highly disciplined outfit. And Lloyd would be the first to acknowledge the debt they owe to English cricket.

New Zealand, of course, have nothing like the natural resources of the West Indies from a cricketing point of view, but they too have grown appreciably stronger through their players' English connections. Captain Geoff Howarth (Surrey), Richard Hadlee (Nottinghamshire) and John Wright (Derbyshire) formed the nucleus of a side that was even capable of beating the West Indies in a somewhat acrimonious series in New Zealand in 1981.

Pakistan, exporting such world-class players as Mushtaq Muhammad, Asif Iqbal, Majid Khan, Zaheer Abbas, Imran Khan and Javed Miandad, and, to a lesser extent, India have also benefited enormously from the English system with the result that many of our administrators, including the Test selectors, believe that most of England's problems can be blamed on the number of overseas players in county cricket.

They have a point in that all the Test-playing countries have gained from the situation apart from England themselves who can argue that the presence of stars like Viv Richards and Joel Garner, Gordon Greenidge and Malcolm Marshall, Clive Rice and Richard Hadlee, Imran Khan and Garth Le Roux, Geoff Howarth and Sylvester Clarke have meant fewer opportunities for young English-born batsmen and, more significantly, fast bowlers.

The Test and County Cricket Board is in the process of trying to restrict the counties to one overseas player each and despite some resistance, most noticeably from Somerset (to no one's surprise!), I am sure they will succeed in the end. Yet, all things considered, I do not believe the influx of 'foreigners' has been a bad thing.

For years, the County Championship was dominated by Yorkshire (champions 31 times) and Surrey (cham-

150

pions 18 times) but in recent years it has been far more evenly contested with the title going to Hampshire, Worcestershire, Leicestershire, Middlesex, Kent, Essex and Nottinghamshire in the past decade. Somerset have still not managed to win it but their success in the one-day game means they have been making the kind of profits they never even dreamed about before the introduction of overseas players.

On balance, then, they have probably done more good than harm. And I believe the powers-that-be should be looking in other directions to discover the real reasons for the decline in England's fortunes – especially on tour.

Until David Gower's team surprised everyone by over-coming all kinds of problems to win 2–1 in India in 1984–85, England had lost successive Test series in Australia, the West Indies, India, Australia again, New Zealand and Pakistan, winning only one match in the process!

Obviously teams are at a great advantage playing on their own grounds in front of their own crowds and, I need hardly add, with their own umpires. Pakistan, for instance, are almost as difficult to beat in their own country as the West Indies are in the Caribbean – yet after thrashing Australia on the sub-continent they found the roles reversed as soon as they went 'down under'. Similarly, England had no great problem overcoming New Zealand at home in 1983, yet within months were losing to virtually the same side in New Zealand.

Yet for all the problems facing them overseas, one has to wonder how much thought goes into an England tour. Look at the ill-fated trip to New Zealand and Pakistan in the winter of 1983/4. It began with two 'warm-up' matches in Fiji – which were certainly warm but no use to anybody as preparation for what lay ahead. Then there were just three first-class games in New Zealand before the first Test and only one more before the remaining two Tests and three one-day internationals. Finally it was on to Pakistan where there was no cricket at all in between the three Test matches and two one-day internationals.

No wonder we lost both series. It was an absurd, ill-

151

arranged tour, giving the players little or no chance of getting into any sort of form. Only the players should be the last to complain – for to pay them what they now demand for overseas tours has meant scrapping the minor matches which give them the kind of practice they need but attract relatively small crowds in favour of a string of one-day games which virtually guarantee big attendances and much-needed revenue.

It is all a question of balance. Naturally everyone involved wants to make as much money as possible but they also have a responsibility to produce good cricket. And it is high time that the International Cricket Conference – the ruling body made up of representatives of all the Test-playing countries – tackled the problem. While we are waiting for them to do that (which could be a long time since the ICC has become something of a joke because of its apparent inability to make any kind of decision about even the most mundane matters, never mind the important issues) the Test and County Cricket Board should set about putting its own house in order to give England a more realistic chance of success.

They should start by appointing a team manager which would have the immediate effect of making the England set-up far more professional, especially in the all-important matter of team selection. To be perfectly frank about it, the existing policy of having five selectors sitting down with the captain to pick the side is old hat in this day and age. Very few people have the time to watch cricket day in and day out in this country, let alone make themselves available to travel overseas for up to four months at a stretch. And the fortunate few who are in that position do not have the qualifications for the job.

Consider the situation in 1984. England needed the best players available for every position to stand any chance at all against the West Indies, easily the strongest team in the world. Yet if you had conducted a referendum among the country's professional cricketers, you would have come up with a rather different side from the ones the selectors picked.

Take the spin bowling, for instance. The selectors chose

Nick Cook and Geoff Miller for the first Test at Edgbaston – which England lost by an innings and 180 runs – yet few of the professionals would have considered them the leading exponents of left-arm and off spin respectively. Most would have gone for Phil Edmonds and Pat Pocock – and so would I.

It was a mystery to me why the selectors continued to ignore Pocock even after John Emburey, his only superior, had been banned for three years for taking part in the rebel tour of South Africa. And the omission of Edmonds could only be put down to a clash of temperaments between him and some of the top players and/or selectors. All I will say about that is that neither of the two great left-arm spinners I played with – Tony Lock and Johnny Wardle – were particularly easy to get on with but it did not stop them playing Test cricket. And in Edmonds's case it was surely only a question of sensible people sitting down and sorting out the problem to stop the sheer waste of his talent.

As far as the quicker bowlers were concerned, a lot of us closely involved with the county game felt the selectors were going crazy because all they ever seemed to talk about was finding fast bowlers when it was quite obvious that the cupboard was bare. We simply did not have a Tyson, a Trueman or a Statham, and it was pointless picking somebody for the simple reason that he could bowl fast if he was not good enough.

Yet there were a few bowlers around in the medium and medium-fast category – people like Lancashire's Paul Allott, Kent's Richard Ellison and Hampshire's Tim Tremlett – who had been steadily improving season by season and should have been under consideration long before England lost the first two Test matches. None of them were speed merchants but they had learned their trade. And if you have not got genuine pace available, you have to pick the next best thing.

What I am saying is that England need somebody at the helm who is very much in touch with the modern game, and not someone whose playing days ended 25 years ago. He should be given full responsibility for running the team, including selection, discipline both on and off the field (with the authority to deal with offenders without reference to half-a-dozen committees at Lord's!), and the organization of tours in consultation with the secretariat.

And to get the right man, the Test and County Cricket Board should offer a realistic salary, which in my view would have to be nothing less than £30,000 a year.

That brings us to the all-important question. Just who is the right man, this supremo who could be trusted by the authorities, accepted by the paying public and, above everything else, respected by the players whose own power these days should never be underestimated? Well, as I write, there are probably only three people in the country whom I would consider suitable.

One is Ray Illingworth, whose failure to solve Yorkshire's problems should not have detracted from his reputation as one of the most knowledgeable men in the game.

Another is Micky Stewart, who, as I can testify from my own experience as chairman of the cricket committee at the Oval, has done a magnificent job as team manager at Surrey, even though some of the results as we began the 1985 season had tended to suggest otherwise.

And the third is Mike Brearley, whose skills as a psychoanalyst would prove more than useful in the England dressing room if he could be tempted back into the game!

The appointment of any one of these three would, I am convinced, at least enable England to get the best out of the talent available, though improving the quality of that talent is quite a different matter which ought to be exercising the mind of every administrator in the game. For it should be obvious by now that the present structure of first-class cricket in this country is just not producing sufficient players of the highest class.

Again, it is all a question of balance. I would be the last person to decry one-day cricket because it has done more than anything else to keep the county clubs alive. But there can be do doubt in anyone's mind that it is never going to be a breeding ground for Test cricketers. It has brought the crowds back to the grounds, boosting gate receipts and attracting sponsors and advertisers to bolster the critical financial position of so many of the counties. And it has raised the standard of outfielding to a level never seen before. On the other hand, it has retarded the progress of middle-order batsmen and produced a generation of medium pacers to the detriment of potential fast bowlers and, saddest of all, spinners.

It is essential, therefore, that instead of tinkering around with the County Championship – the latest idea, in 1984, of bowling a minimum of 117 overs a day (reduced to 112 overs a day for the 1985 season) was quite absurd and often reduced the third day to the level of limited-overs cricket after two days' jostling for position – the Test and County Cricket Board should now carry out a major reconstruction of the English game. And while no formula for improving it is going to be foolproof, I do not think they can do better than implement the programme Surrey have been suggesting for several years.

I can almost hear its critics saying 'here we go again', but I make no apologies for repeating the details of a proposed new fixture structure based on 16 *four-day* matches which has the laudable aims of providing a fair and sensible County Championship, maintaining and improving present financial returns, raising playing standards and consequently improving the performance of the England team, and above all, eliminating the possibility of a drop in public interest in Test cricket through not satisfying the modern demand for success through the highest standards.

This is the suggested format:

The County Championship, currently sponsored by Britannic Assurance, would be a four-day competition played on each Friday, Saturday, Monday and Tuesday.

The John Player Special League would retain its 16-match programme with all matches being played within the relevant Championship fixture to make up a block of five consecutive playing days.

The Benson and Hedges Cup would have a nine-match qualifying competition, played on Thursdays only. There would be two divisions – North and South. Two days would be allocated for the semi-finals with the final played on a Saturday with the following Monday and Tuesday available to complete it if necessary.

The NatWest Trophy would remain the same with the final providing a suitable climax to the season three days after the last championship match and six days after the final Sunday league match.

All fixtures would alternate each week home and away, giving counties six consecutive days' cricket.

Home fixtures of neighbouring counties would probably never clash.

University matches, preferably over three days, would be played in May and June.

The major tourists would play the MCC and between eight and eleven of the counties while other tourists could also be catered for in May and June.

I have no doubt that such a programme would have the desired effect of giving young players far more opportunity to improve their techniques and reach the standard necessary to succeed in Test cricket. For batsmen, there would be many more chances to play long innings and compile big scores, especially in the middle order. For bowlers, there would be much more encouragement to attack which would help the development of genuine pace and spin.

And in general terms, the quality of the game would surely be enhanced with counties having to provide the best possible pitches to last four days, manufactured finishes through declarations being reduced and captaincy improving through the need to be more positive tactically rather than simply containing the opposition and waiting for the inevitable declaration.

It would also bring England into line with all the other Test-playing countries, so at least we would be competing on equal terms. We ought to be ahead. But at the moment we are falling behind.

Index

157